COLLECTED POEMS LESBIA HARFORD

Lesbia Harford (1891–1927) was born Lesbia Venner Keogh at Brighton, Melbourne on 9 April 1891. The daughter of Edmund Keogh and his wife Helen, she suffered from a congenital heart defect that affected her health throughout her short life. In 1900 the Keoghs fell on hard times and in an effort to retrieve the family fortunes Edmund went to Western Australia, where he eventually took up farming. Lesbia was educated at convent schools in Melbourne and Ballarat, but gave up her Catholic faith at a young age. In 1912 she enrolled in law at the University of Melbourne and graduated in 1916 in the same class as (Sir) Robert Menzies. While a student, she became heavily involved in radical politics, forming important, long-lasting relationships with other young socialist activists and intellectuals, including Guido Barrachi and Katie Lush. After graduating, Harford went to work in a clothing factory, where she became involved in unionism and joined the Industrial Workers of the World organisation. She moved briefly to Sydney, where in 1920 she married Patrick John O'Flagharite Fingal Harford, an artist and fellow I.W.W. member, before the couple returned to Melbourne. From 1921 to 1924, she worked on a novel, but did not publish it. She attempted to complete her law qualifications and in 1926 became an articled clerk to a Melbourne barrister but, suffering from tuberculosis in addition to her heart condition, her health deteriorated and she died on 5 July 1927, aged thirty-six. Little of Harford's poetry was published during her lifetime; she preserved her work in handwritten exercise books. Her poetry is mainly known through the posthumous collections edited by Nettie Palmer (1941) and by Marjorie Pizer and Drusilla Modjeska (1985). Her novel *The Invaluable Mystery* was eventually published in 1987.

Oliver Dennis is a violin teacher living in Melbourne. He has contributed regularly to *Australian Book Review*, *The Times Literary Supplement*, *Literary Review*, *PN Review* and *The London Magazine*.

Collected Poems
Lesbia Harford

Edited and introduced by
Oliver Dennis

UWA PUBLISHING

First published in 2014 by
UWA Publishing
Crawley, Western Australia 6009
www.uwap.uwa.edu.au

UWAP is an imprint of UWA Publishing,
a division of The University of Western Australia

THE UNIVERSITY OF
WESTERN AUSTRALIA

This book is copyright. Apart from any fair dealing for the purpose of private study, research, criticism or review, as permitted under the Copyright Act 1968, no part may be reproduced by any process without written permission. Enquiries should be made to the publisher.

The moral right of the author has been asserted.

Copyright collection and introduction © Oliver Dennis 2014

National Library of Australia Cataloguing-in-Publication entry

Harford, Lesbia, 1891–1927, author.

Collected Poems Lesbia Harford / Edited and introduced by Oliver Dennis

ISBN: 9781742585352 (paperback)

Includes index.

Australian poetry—20th century.

Other Authors/Contributors:

Dennis, Oliver, editor.

Dewey Number: A821.2

Cover photograph of Lesbia Harford courtesy of the Mitchell Library, New South Wales.
Typeset by J & M Typesetting
Printed by Lightning Source

This project has been assisted by the Australian Government through the Australia Council, its arts funding and advisory body.

> — such a price
> The Gods exact for song;
> To become what we sing.

>> MATTHEW ARNOLD

CONTENTS

Acknowledgements	xvi
Foreword by Les Murray	xvii
Introduction by Oliver Dennis	xix
A Note on the Selection and Punctuation	xxvii
'I dreamt last night'	1
Little Ships	1
"Rather like an Amazon schooled by Athena"	2
'When day is over'	2
Hero Worship	3
Geisha	3
'This year I have seen autumn with new eyes'	3
A Grown Up Sister	4
In the Public Library	4
'Ay, ay, ay, the lilies of the garden'	5
'Oh hall of music, promise fair'	6
'I must haul up prettiness'	6
'Oh I wish that my hair were as satiny shiny'	7
'People sometimes tease me, saying'	7
Adventurers	8
'I count the days until I see you, dear'	10
'You work all day in the boiling sun'	10
'Some happy people can see and hear him daily'	11
'I'm sorry I'm so young who love you, dear'	11
The Tyrant	11
'Tall trees along the road'	12
'Though I had lost my love'	12
God Speaks	13
'You'll never love me'	13

'On the grass in the oaktree shadow I lie'	14
'Each day'	14
'If thou shouldst change, — become a god for me'	14
'My darling boy' [I]	15
'My darling boy' [II]	15
The Troop-ships	16
'Sad trees, black and brown'	16
'Once in the early morning'	16
Separation	17
'I can't feel the sunshine'	17
After Rain	18
Summer Lightning	19
Birthday	19
A Soul in Flight	19
'You, whom the grave cannot bind'	19
'Oh night, find shelter for him in thy robe'	20
Noli Me Tangere	20
A la bien-aimée	21
'Nay, dear, and must our friendship always be'	21
'They say — priests say —'	21
'Oh, you have given me store of happy days'	22
Lie-a-bed	22
'My mission in the world'	23
'O lovely day'	23
Day's End	24
The Electric Tram to Kew	24
A Sophistical Argument	25
'You are a dream woman'	26
'Dearest, dearest'	26
'Today they made a bonfire'	26
'O Day and Night'	27

Development	27
Weekend at Mt. Dandenong	28
'Verse wov'n of thought'	28
'She hates the North wind'	28
'You and I'	29
'Oh you, my own, who have gone before'	29
'Ours was a friendship in secret, my dear'	30
'Sometimes I watch you, mark your brooding eyes'	30
The Dead Youth	30
'O little year, cram full of duty'	31
'The hot winds wake to life in the sweet daytime'	31
'Somebody brought in lilac'	31
'Now you are dead do you race the wind'	32
'I have three loves who are all most dear'	32
'I have years still in which to grow'	32
'Raging winter wind'	33
'Oh man is great. Be great. Seek loveliness'	33
Deliverance Through Art	34
'Blind eyes have I'	34
To Leslie	35
Hecate's Due	35
The Silent Dead	35
'How are the hours employed I spend with you'	36
'Coloured scraps of paper'	36
'Why does she put me to many indignities'	36
Rossetti's Sea-Spell	37
'I do hate the folk I love'	37
'Oh, oh Rosalie'	37
'O city songs'	38
To an Idealist	39
'To Plato's dictum'	40

'All day long'	40
Ruffs for Hilda Esson	40
'If you have loved a brave story'	41
'O flame that bloweth with the wind'	41
'Once I could say pretty things'	42
'You are more fair than shadows are'	42
'I dare not leave the splendid town'	42
The Immigrant	43
'Child Sun'	44
'Emmie, Emmie Adams'	44
'Today when you went up the hill'	45
'Today I saw'	45
'Cherry plum blossom in an old tin jug'	46
'Each morning I pass on my way to work'	46
'I'd love to have you on a rainy day'	46
'Sitting here daylong'	47
'Green and blue'	47
Fatherless	48
Work-girl's Holiday	48
Periodicity [I]	49
Lawstudent and Coach	49
Periodicity [II]	51
Machinists Talking	51
The Invisible People	52
Closing Time: Public Library	52
The Two Swans	53
'Better than beauty's rose'	53
Machinist's Song	54
'Up in my room on my unmade bed'	54
Body and Soul	55
"Our Vegetable Love"	55

Periodicity	56
'This evening I'm alone'	56
'I was sad'	57
'They are so glad of a young companion'	58
'I saw a flight of sparrows through the air'	58
'O little plum tree in the garden, you're'	58
'The God who made this universe'	59
'He has picked grapes in the sun. Oh, it seems'	59
'The love I look for'	60
'He has a fairy wife'	61
'All through the day at my machine'	61
'Sometimes I wish that I were Helen-fair'	62
'Sometimes I am too tired'	62
'My lovely pixie, my good companion'	63
'Into old rhyme'	63
'Those must be masts of ships the gazer sees'	64
'I have golden shoes'	64
'Now I've been three days'	65
'I found an orchid in the valley fair'	65
A Bad Snap	66
'You may have other loves'	66
'Oh, but September is the month of flowers'	66
Th' Inconstant Moon	67
The Contest	67
'Florence kneels down to say her prayers'	68
'I love to see'	68
'O man, O woman, grievest so?'	69
'Over your dear head'	69
'She has all Ireland in her blood'	69
The Melbourne Cup	70
'There is a child's name that I want to say'	70

The Nuns and the Lilies	71
'I have no force to hold my love'	72
'I am afraid'	72
'I'm like all lovers, wanting love to be'	72
'I used to be afraid to meet'	73
'I love a little boy'	74
Buddha in the Workroom	74
Skirt Machinist	75
Dilectus meus	75
'We climbed that hill'	76
'I have to make a soul for one'	80
'Under the pier'	80
A Blouse Machinist	81
An Improver	82
Mortal Poems	82
Beauty and Terror	83
Grotesque	83
Beauty's Fires	84
'This is a pretty road'	84
'Once I thought my love was worth the name'	85
'You want a lily'	85
'Tonight when woes are manifold'	86
'Pink eucalyptus flowers'	86
Rebels	87
'I came to live in Sophia Street'	87
'Every night I hurry home to see'	87
A Scrapheap	88
'I thought I heard something move in the house'	88
'Today is rebels' day. And yet we work'	88
'To look across at Moira gives me pleasure'	89
Street Music	89

'I dreamt last night of happy home-comings'	90
'He looks in my heart and the image there'	90
'My window pane is broken'	91
'Sometimes I think the happiest of love's moments'	91
'O sweet and fair! These words are mine to use'	92
'The people have drunk the wine of peace'	92
Girl's Love	93
'I went down to post a letter'	93
'I must be dreaming through the days'	93
Slayers of Love	94
'When I get up to light the fire'	95
'Today, in class'	95
'One day she put two arms around me'	96
'I bought a red hat'	96
Miss Mary Fairfax	96
'Whenever I think of you, you are alone'	97
A Strike Rhyme	97
'In this little school'	98
'A lady and I were walking'	98
Three Teachers	99
'Now all the lovely days are past'	100
Inventory	100
At Woolongong!	101
One Man's Meat	101
Shop Keeper and Customer	101
A Parlourmaid	102
'When I go up to work the young blue sea'	104
'I used to have dozens of handkerchiefs'	104
Learning Geography	105
To E.B.	105
'I'd like to spend long hours at home'	106

G.B.	106
'I want this thing and that'	106
Wind at Night	107
'I have put off myself awhile'	107
Lovers Parted [I]	108
'Most people have a way of making friends'	108
The Psychological Craze	109
Lovers Parted [II]	110
Appearances	111
About Trees	111
A Deity	112
Martha	112
New Window, St John's Hawksburn	113
'I could not change the world at all'	113
'They sent me pictures of the saints'	114
"All Knowledge …"	114
'How funny it would be if dreamy I'	115
'Pat wasn't Pat last night at all'	115
'A bunch of lilac and a storm of hail'	115
The Changing Hills	116
'O you, dear trees, you have learned so much of beauty'	116
'Last night, in a dream, I felt the peculiar anguish'	117
White Sunshine	117
'Charles Lamb blasts out his litany of names'	118
Flowers and Light	118
A Bronte Legend	118
Pruning Flowering Gums	119
Polytheist	120
"Love is not love …"	121
'I have a beautiful house'	122
The Moonlit Room	122

'I hate work so'	123
The Sisters	124
A Meaning Learnt	124
The Wife	125
Raiment	125
'There is no need of hurrying'	126
'When I am articled'	126
'When my lover put the sea between us'	127
'I read a statement in a newspaper'	128
'I have two loves to learn'	128
Love Celestial	129
'I am no mystic. All the ways of God'	129
'What were the good of stars if none looked on them'	130
A Prayer to Saint Rosa	130
Notes on the Poems	131
Index of Titles	132

ACKNOWLEDGEMENTS

My thanks to: Lidija Haas; Kim Holburn; Rosanne Hunt; Les Murray; Michael Schmidt; Eric Timewell; the Mitchell Library, State Library of New South Wales; Terri-ann White and the staff at UWAP.

FOREWORD

Our Poem of World War I

A third of the way through her short writing life, Lesbia Harford, then still named Keogh, wrote an autobiographical poem titled 'Fatherless':

> I've had no man
> To guard and shelter me,
> Guide and instruct me
> From mine infancy.
>
> No lord of earth
> To show me day by day
> What things a girl should do
> And what she should say.
>
> I have gone free
> Of manly excellence
> And hold their wisdom
> More than half pretence.
>
> For since no male
> Has ruled me or has fed,
> I think my own thoughts
> In my woman's head.

It is possible that the poet's father, Edmund Keogh, played less of a part than his socially more advanced wife, Helen, in choosing their daughter's prophetic Christian name. It is also possible that, in the constrained atmosphere of 1900, a conventional man might have come to feel uncomfortable in a strong female household. His flight from financial woes to settle in Western Australia without his family has a look of escape about it, though one shouldn't speculate too far. Readers who discover Harford's poetry and delight in its ease with love affairs with either sex – so untypical of verse from the early twentieth century – quickly come to see that name Lesbia as a one-word explanation of her muse, but not of how she got away with her honesty. The answer to that lies in lack of publication during her lifetime. Bisexuality, like lesbianism, was never illegal but, like other kinds of gay writing, it had to wait for posterity to furnish unconstrained readers, even in the grimly revolutionary circles Harford frequented.

I consider Ms Harford – I can't bring myself to call her plain 'Harford', as if she were a criminal – as one of the two finest female poets so far seen in Australia; the other has to be Judith Wright. The Melbourne writer has the greater range, with her sprightly pen portraits of fellow workers, her pictorial genius with subjects such as pruning flowering eucalypts, her piercing sorrow at the death of Australian soldiers at the War, her arguably superior ability to reason in verse, as in 'I'm like all lovers, wanting love to be' and several other poems on the traps and imprisonings of love. Her religious poetry, plentiful in one who had forsworn her faith, typically invokes the saints, while Judith Wright has mystical poems of most unearthly intensity. Lesbia Harford is typical of most poets of her time in rarely touching on set radical topics, such as the Aborigines; her idealism tends to be broad-gauged and conventional. She is perhaps to be smiled at for her loathing of fat people, whether or not named Fairfax. Judith Wright is kinder to physical stereotypes, and hardly uses them at all; she is also more awake to the mythic dimension, especially of bush folk. I do consider Lesbia Harford's 'Ours was a friendship in secret, my dear' the finest Australian poem of World War I. I can never read it aloud without choking up.

Finally, I would point to her lyrical gift, so plentifully illustrated in Mr Dennis's splendid compendium. It is said that Ms Harford at times sang her poems aloud, memorably on the Manly ferry when she moved to Sydney; if so, this was one of the few public airing her lyrics got. In the great wealth of short texts she composed, she is occasionally twee, but a great 'unstraining' effort to think freshly bears frequent treasure, as in 'The Invisible People' ('shut in the silent buildings at eleven / they toil to make life meaningless for you') or the rare mentions of her lover's child faraway in Hungary, or of her sometimes violent husband who 'wasn't Pat last night at all'.

LES MURRAY

INTRODUCTION

Critical recognition can be a long time coming. Lesbia Harford (1891–1927) has occupied only a small place in Australian literary history – for decades, she was utterly forgotten – yet when she died, at thirty-six, she left behind three notebooks containing some of the finest lyric poems ever written in Australia:

> Ours was a friendship in secret, my dear,
>   Stolen from fate.
> I must be secret still, show myself calm
>   Early and late.
>
> "Isn't it sad he was killed!" I must hear
>   With a smooth face.
> "Yes, it is sad." — Oh, my darling, my own,
>   My heart of grace.

The flavour, though distinctly local, is hard to pin down. Quiet yet firm, direct yet ambivalent, Harford's writing is striking in its refusal to please, to be anything other than itself. It looks both forwards and backwards, blending Pre-Raphaelite influences and plain-speaking with unusual subtlety. At the same time, Harford was bound inextricably to the period in which she lived: war in Europe, changing attitudes to religion, the suffrage movement, and widespread social upheaval all helped make her one of the first truly modern, urban figures in Australian poetry. Whereas many poets of the time – Mary Gilmore or Banjo Paterson, for example – wrote with an eye to establishing an Australian literature, Harford clearly never gave a moment's thought to abstract notions of culture or nationhood – hence, perhaps, the years of neglect. She instead found her place out of view, where she was free to articulate a distinctive brand of pure, incidental song.[1] Her sole aim was to be true to her own experience, and as a result her poetry resists classification: neither simply 'literary' nor 'popular' in conception, it operates somewhere between the two.

---

[1] Harford is said to have sung her poems aloud, memorably on the Manly ferry.

The seeming slightness of her writing has not helped its cause. Harford had a keen aesthetic sense, but no real belief in the importance of art, as such – life and feeling mattered more to her. She enjoyed brass bands, and was content to remain on the fringes of Melbourne's literary circles, through her friendships with Frank Wilmot and Nettie Palmer. What is more, Harford did not try to build a reputation: she kept her poems to herself as a rule, and was better known for her social and political activism. She published very little in her lifetime, apparently never quite regarding herself as a poet – only as someone who wrote poetry. As she explained, late in life, to the anthologist Percival Serle, refusing permission for one of her poems: 'Your anthology will be read in many places for many years. I would not care to be recalled to the memory of distant friends by the poem you have chosen ... You see, I take my poetry seriously and I am in no hurry to be read'. In 1941, a small selection appeared, assembled by Nettie Palmer, but another forty-four years elapsed before the publication of a more substantial volume, *The Poems of Lesbia Harford* (1985), edited by Drusilla Modjeska and Marjorie Pizer. (I am indebted to Modjeska and Pizer, who first researched Harford's life and poetry, for the biographical details that follow.)

The available material is enlightening, as far as it goes. Harford, the eldest of four children, was born Lesbia Venner Keogh, in Melbourne, into a fairly well-to-do Catholic family (there were distant aristocratic connections on her mother's side). Her father, a financier, was declared bankrupt and disinherited when she was nine or ten. He began to drink, and after he left the family to work as a labourer on Western Australia's rabbit-proof fence, they rarely saw him. By all accounts a strong and resourceful woman, Harford's mother ran a boarding house, and took on a variety of jobs to keep her daughter at convent schools until she matriculated. Harford went on to study law at the University of Melbourne, becoming one of its first female graduates.

Her early poems explore themes of independence and free love, openly referring to her bisexuality; her two most significant relationships during this period were with Katie Lush, her philosophy tutor, and Guido Barrachi, a fellow law student and Marxist. In most of the surviving photographs, Harford, small and dark-haired, has a determined, knowing expression. She suffered from a debilitating heart condition that made her lips appear blue, but she was strong-willed and had a powerful social conscience, choosing law as a matter of principle. As a child, Harford had shown an interest in the work of her mother's ancestor, the social philosopher Benjamin Kidd, and grew up keenly aware of the arbitrary nature of class distinctions. Despite her physical frailty, she set out after graduation to experience ordinary working conditions, and worked for a number of years in clothing factories and as a domestic servant: even in a climate of bluestockingism, the extent of her practical commitment to social justice was unusual. She joined the socialist organisation the Industrial Workers of the World (or 'Wobblies'), and ran anti-conscription meetings, risking prison with hard labour. When the I.W.W. folded around 1920, she chose not to follow other members into the Communist Party.

In 1918, after her affair with Barrachi had ended, Harford moved to Sydney to live with the wife of a jailed activist, and undertook teaching and clerical work, possibly all her health would allow. She was then briefly married to Pat Harford, a working-class war veteran and amateur painter, with whom she moved back to Melbourne. He could be violent when drunk, but it appears they were intermittently happy. Around this time, Harford wrote her only novel, *The Invaluable Mystery*, about the treatment of Germans and radicals in Australia during the war (the manuscript disappeared for more than sixty years, and was first published in 1987). By 1925, Harford was again living with her mother, the marriage over. She was articled to a firm of solicitors the following year, but found the work a strain, and her health deteriorated. She died from the combined effects of pulmonary tuberculosis and a bacterial infection of the heart on 5 July 1927, at St Vincent's Hospital. It was a painful death, according to her brother.

Harford's earliest surviving poem dates from 1908. The startling, unguarded simplicity of her voice is evident from the outset, and in a few years finds its full range:

>Tall trees along the road,
>I never saw you
>Last year in summertime.
>He came before you
>   With his blue eyes.

Warm wind along the road,
I never knew you
Last year in summertime.
We could outdo you
              With our hot sighs.

This year, oh wind and trees,
We're friends together.
Else should I be alone
In this sweet weather
              Beneath fair skies.
                (1914)

Those must be the masts of ships the gazer sees
On through the little gap in the park trees
So far away that seeing almost fails.
Those must be masts, — the lovely masts of ships
Stripped bare of sails.

There's nothing here to please the seeing eyes, —
Four poles with crossway beams against the skies.
But beauty's not for sight. True beauty sings
Of latent movement to the unsensed soul
In love with wings.
              (1917)

The lyrical mode Harford chose to adopt is especially remarkable in the context of a nation still striving to fashion itself. Her verse is littered with folk elements and lyric conventions (repetition, symmetry and antiphony). Yet colouring the whole is streetwise level-headedness that makes the Victorianisms seem incidental. At different times, Harford's poems recall those of Shakespeare, Keats, Emily Dickinson and Edna St Vincent Millay, among others; never grandiose or overblown, they are by turns passionate, prosaic, and faintly 'antique'. The poet's evasiveness, her feeling for life's mutability, directs much of the phrasing, resulting in non-linear, lacunae-filled poems that seem to hang in the air.

Twinned with Harford's love of truth and freedom was an attachment to wildness and undeformed beauty: her poetry often situates some personal drama against a backdrop of elemental forces – sea, wind, sky and rain. The form of her poems sometimes reflects that romantic inclination: just as she tried in life to avoid being pigeonholed or fixed in place, Harford seems not to have wanted her work to feel too finished. The early verse in particular can be made up of disparate strands that refuse to coalesce. Not simply lack of judgement, the effect was apparently deliberate. Note the intimate, yet resolute, quality of Harford's voice when it switches, abruptly, to her own point of view:

> Today they made a bonfire
> Close to the cherry tree
> And smoke like incense drifted
> Through the white tracery.
>
> I think the gardener really
> Played a tremendous game,
> Offering beauty homage
> In soft blue smoke and flame.

An unnameable quality in her writing resembles that found in the poetry of John Shaw Neilson, in many ways her nearest poetic relative. To an extent no longer possible in England or America, the work of both poets remained largely untouched by sophisticated external influences, and operated within a tradition of song-making, though, intriguingly, Harford's poems have something of the disjointed or 'between' quality that T. S. Eliot diagnosed, at around the same time, as a symptom of modernity. Harford also shared Shaw Neilson's gift for examining small, forgotten subjects in a way that lends her poetry an unusually well-developed sense of continuity – her choice of subject matter was, to some degree, simply a peg for purity of utterance. Over seventeen years or so, she drew material from whatever happened to be going on in her life at the time. Certain themes recur, prominent among them being the various conditions of love:

> I lie in the dark
> Grass beneath and you above me,

xxiii

Curved like the sky,
Insistent that you love me.

But the high stars
Admonish to refuse you
And I'm for the stars
Though in the stars I lose you.

('Girl's Love')

Her poetry frequently plays on conflicting desires of wanting to be wanted and wanting to be strong and apart. Harford often portrays love as an agony she longs to escape – Shaw Neilson's references to 'riotous spring' and 'the unfreedom of spring' describe something similar. The phrase 'riotous spring' also turns up in one of her own poems, suggesting a possible familiarity with the older poet's work. One of the many similarities between the two poets is their traditional use of floral imagery to symbolise emotional states: Harford tends to refer to the lilac when evoking experience ('The lilac is companioned by the gale ... Mine are the storms of spring, but not the sweets') and the lily when evoking purity, although to some extent this oversimplifies the many-sided aspects of her symbolism. There are spiritual affinities as well: both poets abandoned formal religion in favour of a freer poetic mysticism. Harford makes use of religious imagery, but in a characteristically agnostic way. Like Shaw Neilson, she developed a spiritual appreciation of colour:

Green and blue
First-named of colours believe these two.
They first of colours by men were seen
This grass colour, tree colour,
Sky colour, sea colour,
Magic-named, mystic-souled, blue and green.

Harford, however, was a grittier and more direct poet than Shaw Neilson, who could never have contented himself with lines like 'I went down to post a letter' or 'I like my kitchen with its pots and pans'. The unusual habit of making affectless statements somehow resonant and allusive is typical of the poetry in general, as is the hint of a defiant adolescent narcissism. Exploring everyday subjects in factual detail, Harford remained true to her egalitarian principles, while managing to produce poetry that speaks to the reader at another level. Thus she evokes the keenly particular atmosphere of a vanished Melbourne, shown here with a characteristic instance of her knack for dialogue and exemplary use of the Sapphic docked line:

> "I used to have dozens of handkerchiefs
> Of finest lawn.
> I used to have silk shirts and fine new suits."
> He's like a faun
>
> This darling out-at-elbows Irish boy.
> "Those were the days
> Before the war
> When money could be earned a thousand ways.
>
> But now, — last week I had a muslin bag
> For handkerchief!
> No socks, no shirts", — but wiles and smiles and gleams
> Beyond belief.

Naturally, Harford also documented her experience in the factories, and wrote satires on oppression and inequality ('Every day Miss Mary goes her rounds, / Through the splendid house and through the grounds …'). Her work, like Beatrix Potter's, intimates a longing to escape constraints. In many poems, she seems to see herself as a kind of secular visionary, who has transformed the pain and loneliness of her father's abandonment into a radical intellectual independence: 'I am no mystic,' she explains in one of her last poems, 'My every act has reference to *man*' (emphasis added). In 'Fatherless', she writes:

> I have gone free
> of manly excellence
> And hold their wisdom
> More than half pretence.

> For since no male
> Has ruled me or has fed,
> I think my own thoughts
> In my woman's head.

While Harford was critical of polemic in poetry – and tried to keep it out of her work – she can sound strident occasionally. A note of assertiveness in her voice became more persistent over time, as she grew in confidence as a poet. There is also a loss of freshness in some of the later poems, coinciding with marriage and the period when she was working on her novel. Around 1922, her poetry begins to make greater use of religious and mystical material. Harford always knew she would probably die young, and it is hard not to conclude from this shift in her work that the reality had begun to seem inescapable.

The question of what she would have written, had she lived, remains tantalising. In a letter, Harford looked forward to revising her poems in old age (she might also have gone on to devote more time to fiction). Possibly, her best work was already behind her when she died. Hers is somehow a poetry of youthful joys and certainties, sorrows and enthusiasms – Harford didn't live long enough to begin to question them. She can be an easy poet to dismiss – the best poems are sometimes hard to find – but read with the uncritical patience of a child, her qualities slowly come into view. Of course, her distinctiveness as a writer had its origins in her contradictions; Harford's was the natural idiom of someone who wanted to sing to the depths of her experience – and of its surfaces – but couldn't find the words: 'So much in life remains unsung', as a late poem has it, 'I'd like a song of kitchenmaids / With steady fingers and swift feet'. As happens sooner or later with all true poets, her poetry's faults have come to seem less important than its qualities, which are at last very much to the fore. In some of her loveliest lines, Lesbia Harford described something similar:

> This year I have seen autumn with new eyes,
> Glimpsed hitherto undreamt of mysteries
> In the slow ripening of the town-bred trees …

OLIVER DENNIS

A NOTE ON THE SELECTION AND PUNCTUATION

In preparing this edition, I have set out to collect all of Lesbia Harford's poetry of value. Of the nearly four hundred poems in manuscript, just over half that number are reproduced here; of these, a third or so – excluding a small selection made for *PN Review* – have not, to my knowledge, appeared in print previously.

The arrangement of the poems is chronological, spanning Harford's all too brief adulthood (the first poem in the book dates from August 1910, the last from January 1927, five months before her death). Harford's output and poetic development over this period follow a natural arc – like most poets, she tended to write well when she was writing a lot. Her most productive years were 1915 and 1917, the former notable for a number of poems in which she mourns the loss of a soldier to whom she had been close. Significantly, in the same year, Harford produced some of her purest and most representative poetry. After 1917, her productivity steadily decreased until her death.

A word on punctuation. Throughout her notebooks (held in the Mitchell Library in Sydney), Harford uses a comma and dash together to indicate parenthesis, a pause or an abrupt change of thought (she seems to have picked up the device from Keats, and, interestingly, Millay used it as well). Where previous editors dispensed with the comma, I have preserved Harford's usage on the basis that it meant something particular to her. Indeed, her use of punctuation was on the whole deliberate and sophisticated – she knew what she was doing. The reader has to remember, too, that, although Harford may have had an eye on posthumous recognition for her poetry, she was not immediately concerned with how it would look in print; inevitably, a handwritten dash and a printed one do not quite mean the same thing.

In other respects, I have adhered to Harford's manuscripts wherever possible, making only occasional alterations for clarity and sense. Inconsistencies, when they appear, are the poet's own.

'I dreamt last night'

I dreamt last night
That spring had come.
Across green fields I saw a blur
Of crimson-blossomed plum.

I've never known
So fair a thing.
And yet I wish it were a dream
Of some forgotten spring.

Today the sun
Our workroom blest
And there was hard young wattle pinned
On our forewoman's breast.

Little Ships

The little ships are dearer than the great ships
For they sail in strange places,
They lean nearer the green waters.
One may count by wavelets how the year slips
From their decks; and hear the Sea-King's daughters
Laughing at their play whene'er the boat dips.

"Rather like an Amazon schooled by Athena"

Down by the river head she was standing,
One of a group of girls disbanding:
Queen of the Amazons, of mien commanding,
          With beauty and splendour crowned.

Out in the pasture-land she was standing,
Chief of a group of girls disbanding;
Schooled by Athena in her weapon's handling,
          To service of wisdom bound.

'When day is over'

When day is over
I climb up the stair
Take off my dark dress
Pull down my hair

Open my window
And look at the stars.
Then my heart breaks through
These prison bars

Of space and darkness
And finds what is true
Up past the stars where
I'm one with you.

Hero Worship

How glad the windows are,
When the dear sun shineth.
They strive to reflect the sun,
To be bright like the sun,
To give heat like the sun.
My heart too has its chosen one,
And so to shine designeth.

Geisha

All the pretty poplar trees have robed themselves in silver,
Like the clouds and like the waves they've clothed themselves
    with light.
Now they're singing songs to me. Maybe across the river
Sister trees sing just such songs for Katie's ears tonight.

'This year I have seen autumn with new eyes'

This year I have seen autumn with new eyes,
Glimpsed hitherto undreamt of mysteries
In the slow ripening of the town-bred trees; —
Horse-chestnut lifting wide hands to the skies;
And silver beech turned gold now winter's near;
And elm, whose leaves like little suns appear
Scattering light, — all, all have made me wise
And writ me lectures in earth's loveliness,
Whether they laugh through the grey morning mist,
Or by the loving sun at noon are kissed
Or seek at night the high-swung lamp's caress.
Does autumn such a novel splendour wear
Simply because my love has yellow hair?

A Grown Up Sister

I'm lying here in bed thinking of you.
You're away dancing.
I wonder who it is you're talking to,
At whom you're glancing.

I'm lying dreaming here and smiling too.
I need no pity,
Yet I wish I were there looking at you.
You are so pretty.

In the Public Library

Standing on tiptoe, head back, eyes and arm
Upraised, Kate groped to reach the higher shelf.
Her sleeve slid up like darkness in alarm
At gleam of dawn. Impatient with herself
For lack of inches, careless of her charm,
She strained to grasp a volume; then she turned
Back to her chair, an unforgetful Eve
Still snatching at the fruit for which she yearned
In Eden. She read idly to relieve
The forehead where her daylong studies burned,
Tales of an uncrowned queen who fed her child
On poisons, till death lurked, in act to spring,
Between the girl's breasts; who with soft mouth smiled,
With soft eyes tempted the usurping King
Then dealt him death in kisses. Kate had piled
Her books three deep before her and across
This barricade she watched an old man nod
Over a dirty paper, until loss
Of life seemed better than possession. Shod
With kisses death might skid like thistle floss
Down windy slides, might prove at heart as gay
As Cinderella in glass slippers.
Life goes awkwardly so sandalled. Had decay

Been the girl's gift in that Miltonic strife
She would have rivalled God, Kate thought. A ray
Of sunshine, carrying gilded flecks of dust
And minutes bright with fancies, touched her hair
To powder it with gold and silver, just
As if being now admitted she should wear
The scholar's wig, colleague of those whose lust
For beauty hidden in an outworn tongue
Had made it possible for her to read
Tales that were fathered in Arabia, sung
By trouvères and forgotten with their creed
Of love and magic. Beams that strayed among
Kate's fingers lit a rosy lantern there
To glow in twilight. Suddenly afraid
She seemed to see her beauty in a flare
Of light from hell. A throng of devils swayed
Before her, devils that had learned to wear
The shape of scholar, poet, libertine.
They smiled, frowned, beckoned, swearing to estrange
Kate from reflection that her soul had been
Slain by her woman's body or would change
From contact with it to a thing unclean.
Woman was made to worship man, they preached,
Not God, to serve earth's purpose, not to roam
The heavens of thought … A factory whistle screeched,
Someone turned up the lights. On her way home
Kate wondered in what mode were angels breeched.

'Ay, ay, ay, the lilies of the garden'

Ay, ay, ay, the lilies of the garden
With red threads binding them and stars about,
These shall be her symbols, for she is high and holy,
Holy in her maidenhood and very full of doubt.

Ay, ay, ay, for she is very girlish,
Fearful her heart's lilies should be stained by sin.
Yet will I bind them with rosy threads of passion.
Surely human passion has a right to enter in.

'Oh hall of music, promise fair'

Oh hall of music, promise fair,
No memories yet to thee belong.
No ghostlings hover in thine air
Of nights made sweet with song.

Oh stately hall in coming years
May harmony, the heavenly norm,
Here ever sounding in our ears
Rouse us to world reform.

'I must haul up prettiness'

I must haul up prettiness
From the depths of hell
If I'm of a mind to make
John love me well.

I must pull down holiness
From the heights of heaven
If I wish that unto me
Johnny's love be given.

'Oh I wish that my hair were as satiny shiny'

Oh I wish that my hair were as satiny shiny
As blessed St Magdalen's ages ago,
For then my new ribbon would glitter more bravely
Than all the fine jewels that a princess can show.
                And Johnny would love me,
                And praise my new ribbon.
                Ah, would it were so!

Oh I wish that my eyes were not green as the rushes
Where deep in the river the sturdiest grow,
With blue skies above them, — that rare and sweet colour.
If my eyes were blue, he would praise them I know.
                My Johnny would praise them
                And close them with kisses.
                Ah, would it were so!

'People sometimes tease me, saying'

People sometimes tease me, saying
I have lovers many.
If I lack the one I sigh for,
What's the good of any?

I will never have a lover,
Though I am so bonny.
Love could only hurt that showed me
What I miss from Johnny.

Adventurers

This morning I got up before the sun
Had seized the hill,
And scrambled heart-hot, noisy, past each one
In sleep laid still.

There they lay helpless under the gold stars,
Good folk and kind,
By sleep the robber spoiled of heavenly wares,
Made deaf and blind.

The leaves cracked, the grass rustled as I passed.
I might have been
Myself the thief. Each minute seemed the last
Of freedom's teen.

But lonely down the hill in Levite's guise
Or priest's, I ran.
I had not proved myself, true loverwise,
Samaritan.

The wind went by me, pulling at my hair.
I left the track.
My last night's purpose terrible and fair
Came sweeping back.

Among the bracken under a white tree
I sat me down,
And slipped my shoulders very stealthily
From out my gown.

One minute I lay naked on the grass,
Then sat upright.
The hot wind had its will with me, and kissed
My bosom white.

The stars gleamed in the grey before the rose.
Were they not eyes
That peered and leered, and seemed about to close
In shocked surprise?

With the whole sky at gaze, there had I lain,
Had dared thus much.
I ran on frightened down the hill again,
With gown to clutch.

Down by the creek the blackberries grew thick,
And as I passed
They stretched long arms, — to hinder me and prick,
Make me shamefast?

Nay, they laughed, pulling at my slipping gown,
Would have laid bare
To chance men on the hillside looking down
The whiteness there.

Close by the blackwoods is the bathing pool
The men have made.
I was no sport for stars, no bramble's fool
In the trees' shade.

But when I stood with limbs and body free
And gleaming fair,
The little kind ferns screened and covered me
Like Agnes' hair.

I slipped into the shallow water, felt
The fine brown sand
Of the creek bottom, shuddered, splashed and knelt
Too cold to stand.

Happy and shivering, with trees overhead,
Fern walls around,
I listened to the water talking, led
To praise by sound.

So I have felt the wind and water's kiss,
Though I'm a maid.
Better be man than be a girl, and miss
Feeling afraid.

'I count the days until I see you, dear'

I count the days until I see you, dear,
But the days only.
I dare not reckon up the nights and hours
I shall be lonely.

But when at last I meet you, dearest heart,
How can it cheer me?
Desire has power to turn me into stone,
When you come near me.

I give my heart the lie against my will,
Seem not to see you,
Glance aside quickly if I meet your eye,
Love you and flee you.

'You work all day in the boiling sun'

You work all day in the boiling sun,
Work in the heat and grime.
If many such days should come, beloved,
You'd weary before your time.

I sit at home in the cool and plan
What I'd most like to do, —
Swagger out there in the heat of the sun
And finish your work for you.

'Some happy people can see and hear him daily'

Some happy people can see and hear him daily,
Chosen friends and trusted. Would that I were one.
I can only think of him and long for him and love him,
Love him from the rising to the setting of the sun.

Some happy people can spend the evenings with him.
Softly must the hours step when the gold stars shine.
I can only think of him and long for him and love him.
Plotting still and planning still to make such moments mine.

'I'm sorry I'm so young who love you, dear'

I'm sorry I'm so young who love you, dear.
If I were older
I might write better verses in your praise,
Sweeter and bolder.

Yet had I grown old not knowing you
Or your beseeching,
I could have written nothing. All my songs
Are of your teaching.

The Tyrant

When I was a child,
I felt the fairies' power.
Of a sudden my dry life
Would burst into flower.

The skies were my path,
The sun my comrade fair,
And the night was a dark rose
I wore in my hair.

But thou camest, love,
Who madest me unfree.
I will dig myself a grave
And hide there from thee.

'Tall trees along the road'

Tall trees along the road,
I never saw you
Last year in summertime.
He came before you
   With his blue eyes.

Warm wind along the road,
I never knew you
Last year in summertime.
We could outdo you
   With our hot sighs.

This year, oh wind and trees,
We're friends together.
Else should I be alone
In this sweet weather
   Beneath fair skies.

'Though I had lost my love'

Though I had lost my love,
The hills could calm me.
Deep in a woodland grove
No loss could harm me.

But when I came to town,
And saw around me
Lovers pass up and down, —
Then sorrow crowned me.

God Speaks

I made a heaven for you filled with stars,
Each star a song
Meant to give happy music to your ear,
Day and night long.

But in your workshop you are closed away
From the fair sky,
Deafened by noise until you cannot hear
My stars that sigh.

And when night comes your sleepy eyes are blind
To heaven's blue, —
That was a foolish toy, my dearest dear,
I made for you.

'You'll never love me'

You'll never love me.
All my beseeching
Is powerless to move you;
But you are teaching
One lesson I'd learn, if I could.
"Heigh-ho, but forgetting is good."

If my love faltered,
You would not heed it.
Old wives conjure me
You'll never need it.
Foolish me! I'd forget if I could.
"Heigh-ho, but forgetting is good."

'On the grass in the oaktree shadow I lie'

On the grass in the oaktree shadow I lie.
Through greengold leaves I look at the sky.

As the wind in the branches, tossing the blue,
So in my heart is my love for you.

'Each day'

Each day
Of sky and sea
Bears you from me
Into the crowded distance leagues away.

Worse ill!
As each blue day
Passes away,
Forgetfulness comes tripping nearer still.

'If thou shouldst change, — become a god for me'

If thou shouldst change, — become a god for me,
Then wouldst thou need my prayers to comfort thee.

If thou shouldst fail, weaken, grow childlike say,
Thou wouldst be all my care from day to day.

But thou art young and strong. Oh let me call
This joy a grief! Thou needst me not at all.

'My darling boy' [I]

    My darling boy
    The world wears black
    And everything I do
Seems sorrowful when I'm away from you
    My darling boy.

    My darling boy
    I dream all day
    And stay awake at night
Starwise, and weep lest you forget me quite
    My darling boy.

'My darling boy' [II]

    My darling boy
You have two gold rings on your fingers brown, —
I could kiss the fingers one by one.
Was there ever a soldier under the sun
With golden rings on his fingers, dear?
Solomon, look at the wonder here,
Here is a beauty you have not seen, —
    My darling boy!

    My darling boy
I gave you my brooch for a charm, — a spell,
Pinned it high up on your shoulder, dear,
With its three little pearls, and each pearl a tear,
The strap above, to hide it away.
You wear your rings and my brooch all day
So should you be decked with gold and pearl,
    My darling boy.

The Troop-ships

Up the river in the sun,
We rowed slowly.
Oftentimes the willow boughs
Screened us wholly.
Ours were all the tiny joys
That bless the lowly.

Mighty ships upon the seas
Onward bore you.
Battles dim and agony
Lay before you.
I half-wished our willows spread
Their branches o'er you.

'Sad trees, black and brown'

Sad trees, black and brown,
   In woodland green,
Your unlovely branches show
   Where fire has been.

Round you, slim and sweet,
   The saplings spring.
You must dread the happy songs
   Their young leaves sing.

'Once in the early morning'

Once in the early morning
When the little leaves were astir,
I slithered away from my darling's side
And down to the edge of the sea I hied
That met the sky in a blur.

And I listened an hour to the waves' sweet moan,
And I left my dear love all alone,
For I went to dream of her.

Separation

Here,
I sit rapt on the cliff overlooking the sea,
White sand at my feet, the soft wind blowing free.

There,
Worlds away where you are, in a waterless land
The wind sleeps forever, and gold gleams the sand.

Dear,
Our two worlds are more like than the gods we adore,
For I dream of friendship and you reverence war.

'I can't feel the sunshine'

I can't feel the sunshine
Or see the stars aright
For thinking of her beauty
And her kisses bright.

She would let me kiss her
Once and not again.
Deeming soul essential,
Sense doth she disdain.

If I should once kiss her,
I would never rest
Till I had lain hour long
Pillowed on her breast.

Lying so, I'd tell her
Many a secret thing
God has whispered to me
When my soul took wing.

Would that I were Sappho,
Greece my land, not this!
There the noblest women,
When they loved, would kiss.

After Rain

Today
I'd like to be a nun
And go and say
My rosary beneath the trees out there.
In this shy sun
The raindrops look like silver beads of prayer.

So blest
Am I, I'd like to tell
God and the rest
Of heaven-dwellers in the garden there
All that befell
Last week. Such gossip is as good as prayer.

Ah well!
I have, since I'm no nun,
No beads to tell,
And being happy must be all my prayer.
Yet 'twould be fun
To walk with God 'neath the wet trees out there.

Summer Lightning

Just now, as warm day faded from our sight,
Hosts of archangels, fleet
On lightning-wingèd feet
Passed by, all glimmering in the busy night.

Sweet angels, bring no blinding truth to birth,
Give us no messages
From heavenly palaces;
Leave us our dark trees and our starlight earth.

Birthday

I have a sister whom God gave to me;
He formed her out of trouble and the mists of the sea.

Like Aphrodite, she came to me full-grown.
Oh, I am blest forever with a sister of my own.

A Soul in Flight

Can I not keep you alive,
Must you go roaming
Further than I can follow,
O bee with a star for a hive?
All your flight's but a homing
Sunward, my swallow.

'You, whom the grave cannot bind'

You, whom the grave cannot bind,
  Shall a song hold you?
Still you escape from the mesh
  Spun to enfold you.

Your woven texture of flesh
Short time confined you.
Sib to the sun and the wind,
Shall a song bind you?

'Oh night, find shelter for him in thy robe'

Oh night, find shelter for him in thy robe,
Be loth to free him from thy clinging arms,
Make him thy constant lover; for the days
Are fatal charms.

Oh hills, give easy pathways to his feet,
Yea, little easy paths that climb the sky.
If he should yield him to the valley's love
He must soon die.

Noli Me Tangere

We watched the dawn breaking across the sea
While just above us hung the evening star.
The nearer waters took a hint of white
And clouds and waves together massed afar,
Narrowed our morning world of pallid light
Till dawn seemed very close to you and me.

"Nay, dawn, stay farther off. Be Magdalen.
Go back into the distance whence you came.
The Near is meaningless when Far is nought,"
So I; and you, "Wait but a little then,
And day, whole day, uprising like a flame,
Will show us the far reaches of our thought."

A la bien-aimée

Oh, sunlight on the water's beautiful,
And dawn across wide seas,
And moonlit waves crawling to lick the feet
Of the tall starward trees.

And seven days and nights of beauty, mine.
No more than seven days;
Yet — am I blind to it, oh Lovelier far
Than all these sights I praise.

'Nay, dear, and must our friendship always be'

Nay, dear, and must our friendship always be
A thing of surfaces,
Of laughter lifting,
And light clouds drifting
So far beneath the blue immensity?

We must look past the easy things to see, —
Past tears, past laughter,
Past storms that lower,
Or dawns in flower, —
To find the deep far heart of thee and me.

'They say — priests say —'

They say — priests say —
That God loves the world.
Maybe he does,
When the dew is pearl'd
On the emerald grass,
Or the young dawns shine.
Would you be satisfied,
Proteus mine,

Just to be loved
When your hair was curled,
As Earth is beloved
When Earth is fine?
I love you more
Than God loves the world.

'Oh, you have given me store of happy days'

Oh, you have given me store of happy days
Fondly remembered.
But find a surer proof of love than these
In all the tears I shed.

Lie-a-bed

My darling lies down in her soft white bed,
And she laughs at me.
Her laughter has flushed her pale cheeks with red.
Her eyes dance with glee.

My darling lies close in her warm white bed,
And she will not rise.
I will shower kisses down on her sleepyhead
Till she close her eyes.

Gioja's no happier fresh from the South.
But my kisses free
Will straiten the curves of this teasing mouth,
If it laughs at me.

'My mission in the world'

My mission in the world
Is to prolong
Rapture, by turning it
Into a song.

A song of liberty
Bound by no rule!
No marble meaning's mine
Fixed for a school.

My singing ecstasy
Winged for the flight,
Each will hear differently,
And hear aright.

'O lovely day'

       O lovely day,
Be as kind to my dear as you are to me.
Pour living gold on her golden head,
Stain her, the Flowerlike, rosy red,
Give her young Rapture for company,
       O lovely day.

Day's End

    Little girls,
    You are gay, —
Little factory girls, —
At the end of your day.

    There you stand,
    Huddled close,
On the back of a tram,
Having taken your dose.

    And you go
    Through the gray
And the gold of the streets
At the close of the day,

    Blind as moles.
    You are crude,
You are sweet, — little girls, —
And amazingly rude,

    But so fine
    To be gay.
Gentle people are dull
At the end of the day.

The Electric Tram to Kew

Through the swift night
I go to my love.
Tram bells are joy bells,
Bidding us move
On a golden path
Beneath balls of fire
Up hill and down dale,
To o'ertake desire.

Past the old shops
That my childhood knew,
Past hidden houses
And fields of dew
Lovely and secret
As thou, my friend,
Who art all heaven
At journey's end.

A Sophistical Argument

Great crane o'ertopping the delicate trees
    Why do you seem so fair,
Swaying and raising your load with ease
    High in the misty air?

You are a wonder of pearl and gray
    Lifting strong arms to the sky.
Have you a meaning that's lovely, pray?
    Why are you lovely, why?

I have a friend with a theory strange,
    Thriftless in unity,
None of my reasons avails to change.
    "Beauty *is* truth," says she.

Are you all ugliness, Fair-to-the-sense?
    You are a symbol drear.
Though I should forfeit mine innocence,
    Yet must I hold you dear.

'You are a dream woman'

You are a dream woman
    Beautiful and fair,
With kindness in your bosom
    And stars among your hair.

All the world must love you
    Love and reverence more.
For out of reason have you come
    And through the Future's door.

'Dearest, dearest'

Dearest, dearest,
Bother the slow hours
That hold and keep me
From the leafy bowers
You make more lovely than a storm of flowers.

Dearest, dearest,
If they let me go
I'd hasten to you
Where the waters flow
In among the shadows and the dreams we know.

'Today they made a bonfire'

Today they made a bonfire
Close to the cherry tree
And smoke like incense drifted
Through the white tracery.

I think the gardener really
Played a tremendous game,
Offering beauty homage
In soft blue smoke and flame.

'O Day and Night'

      O Day and Night,
Your slender body is woven of light,
Rosy and gold as a summer's day.

      O Sun and Moon,
Your glimmering soul has learnt the way
Paradise looks through the nights of June.

Development

Your friend writes verses to you
Full of praise,
Singing the beauty
Of your earlier days.

She calls you "more than human,"
And I grow
Heartsick, — my dearest,
Dearest, be not so.

You are my friend more surely
When I praise
Dear imperfections
Of your later days.

Weekend at Mt. Dandenong

Frolic mountain winds
Innocent and shy
Kiss my darling's cheek
As they scurry by.

Little fragrant leaves
With the dawn astir
Make a million songs
Full of love for her.

Will she wake or sleep
These two nights she'll spend
Up the mountain-side,
My dear truant friend?

'Verse wov'n of thought'

Verse wov'n of thought
Is verse that will decay.
The mightiest hymns
Are songs of yesterday.

My verse, that's just
A cry of love, is strong.
Th' eternal years
Renew my living song.

'She hates the North wind'

She hates the North wind,
My golden sister.
When she was a little girl
The South wind kissed her.

He made her young soul
A fragrant garden,
A lovely heaven on earth
Without a warden.

'You and I'

You and I
Live apart, it would seem
To the town folk, who dream
Of dim years flitting by, —
You and I.
You and I
Have a place of our own
Where we dwell, — a heart's home
Up the mountain high, —
You and I.
You and I.

'Oh you, my own, who have gone before'

Oh you, my own, who have gone before,
    You have made me wise.
I look into the heaven, at the beauty there,
    Through your closed eyes.

All things in common we hold, my friend:
    Young and weak we were;
Now in fulfilling of wisdom, I have
    With you, my share.

'Ours was a friendship in secret, my dear'

Ours was a friendship in secret, my dear,
    Stolen from fate.
I must be secret still, show myself calm
    Early and late.

"Isn't it sad he was killed!" I must hear
    With a smooth face.
"Yes, it is sad." — Oh, my darling, my own,
    My heart of grace.

'Sometimes I watch you, mark your brooding eyes'

Sometimes I watch you, mark your brooding eyes,
Your grave brow over-weighted with deep thought,
Your mouth's straight line, — details of such a sort
That all aloofness in your aspect lies.

And yet when in the dark down from above
You swoop like a great bird or God himself
To kiss, your lips have curves. What changeling elf
Is that soft mouth of passionate close love?

The Dead Youth

He was like the morning
Visionary fair, —
When bright clouds go driving
Through the shining air,
And the delicate branches
Toss in storm and rain.
Not a lass who loved him
Ever loved again.

'O little year, cram full of duty'

O little year, cram full of duty,
Rapture and sorrow, too,
Show me the way from old paths of beauty
Into the fields of dew.

Strange lorn fields where the moon goes riding
Over a lonely sky.
Kind little year, in your onward gliding
Let me not pass them by.

'The hot winds wake to life in the sweet daytime'

The hot winds wake to life in the sweet daytime
My weary limbs,
And tear through all the moonlit darkness shouting
Tremendous hymns.

My body keeps earth's law and goes exulting.
Poor slavish thing!
The soul that knows you dead rejects in silence
This riotous spring.

'Somebody brought in lilac'

Somebody brought in lilac, —
Lilac after rain.
Isn't it strange, belovèd of mine,
You'll not see it again?

Lilac glad with the sun on it
Flagrant fair from birth,
Mourns in colour, belovèd of mine,
You laid in the earth.

'Now you are dead do you race the wind'

Now you are dead do you race the wind,
Are you fair and free as the day?
No, ah no, belovèd of mine,
For we are greater than they.

Though you are dead you are human still, —
Fail in the human way.
They are great, the sun and the wind,
But we are greater than they.

'I have three loves who are all most dear'

I have three loves who are all most dear.
Each one has cost me many a tear.

The one who is dead yet lives in me.
I were too poor had I less than three.

'I have years still in which to grow'

I have years still in which to grow,
Age and grow, change and grow.
I must leave the self that you came to know.
                    Leave you so?

Can it be true that you'll not grow?
No and no, no and no.
You are dead. You wouldn't forsake me though,
                    Lose me so.

'Raging winter wind'

"Raging winter wind
Let loose in springtime
What is the message your cold touch brings?"
Spite of days and dreams,
Warm and easy and sublime,
Terror crouches always at the heart of things.

'Oh man is great. Be great. Seek loveliness'

"Oh man is great. Be great. Seek loveliness,
The lasting beauty, and the lasting good.
Doubt is a small thing easily withstood
And nightly conquered. Spirit knows no end."
Such words he spoke, — words strong to heal and bless, —
                              My living friend.

"Man is not great, — not great. This loveliness
Is the best unreality we know,
But 'tis unreal. Fear not to call it so
While seeking it as long as you have breath."
Is this the deeper truth you would impress,
                              My friend in death?

Deliverance Through Art

When I am making poetry I'm good
And happy then.
I live in a deep world of angelhood
Afar from men.
And all the great and bright and fiery troop
Kiss me agen
With love. Deathless Ideas! I have no need
Of girls' lips then.

Goodness and happiness and poetry,
I put them by.
I will not rush with great wings gloriously
Against the sky
While poor men sit in holes, unbeautiful,
Unsouled, and die.
Better let misery and pettiness
Make me their sty.

'Blind eyes have I'

Blind eyes have I
That cannot see.
From morn till night
They search for thee, —
At home, abroad,
In every spot.
Blind eyes have I
That find thee not.

To Leslie

Across the sea
Come homeward ships
With freight of boys.

And still must we
Forgo the joys
Of meeting lips.

Hecate's Due

You who are dead,
Do you know
They've dug up half the irises
That used to grow
Here in the quadrangle a year ago?

Those left are mere
Points of blue
That can't make sky of earth, as once
They used to do,
Didn't they? Buried flowers … Proserpin's due.

The Silent Dead

There's a little boy who lives next door
With hair like you, —
Pale, pale hair and a rose-white skin
And his eyes are blue.

When I get a chance I peep at him,
Who is so like you, —
Terribly like, my dead, my fair,
For he's dumb too.

'How are the hours employed I spend with you'

How are the hours employed I spend with you, —
In talk of incidents that fill the soul
As much and little as such trifles do?

Nay, we are busied with great books, where fears
On lightning certainties like thunder roll
In conflict elemental through the years.

'Coloured scraps of paper'

Coloured scraps of paper
The modern world knows
Blossom for an instant
Like the short-lived rose.

Tram-cheques and Train-tickets,
Squares of blue and red,
Shall we keep them longer
Than the lovely dead?

'Why does she put me to many indignities'

Why does she put me to many indignities,
Shifts to prevent myself thinking upon her,
My golden Katie, who loveth not kisses?

I wear my new dresses and put on silk stockings,
All to prevent myself thinking upon her,
Who is more lovely than fair river-lilies.

Rossetti's Sea-Spell

The man who painted this is dead today
As Leslie is, — and yet how differently!
He left great pictures for the world to see
While Leslie left an image in one heart,
One only heart that may inconstant prove.
O heart, be strong and let the gazers know
There is no beauty like enduring love.

'I do hate the folk I love'

I do hate the folk I love,
They hurt so.
Their least word and act may be
Source of woe.

"Won't you come to tea with me?"
"Not today.
I'm so tired, I've been to church,"
Such folk say.

All the dreary afternoon
I must clutch
At the strength to love like them, —
Not too much.

'Oh, oh Rosalie'

Oh, oh Rosalie,
Oh, oh Rosalie,
What would you have of me?
Oh, oh Rosalie.

I have kisses fine,
I have kisses fine.
Will you take kiss of mine?
Oh, oh Rosalie.

I have dreams in store,
I have dreams in store,
Fine spun as lace of yore.
Oh, oh Rosalie.

Many a mighty thought,
Many a mighty thought
By men of old time wrought
Is mine, Rosalie.

I have golden days,
I have golden days,
Green trees, and leafy ways.
Oh, oh Rosalie.

I have tears for you,
I have tears for you,
And roses filled with dew.
Oh, oh Rosalie.

Oh, oh Rosalie,
What do you want of me?
You would have nought of me.
Oh, oh Rosalie.

'O city songs'

O city songs,
Little grimy songs,
My girl's beauty
How shall you discover?

Like little boys,
Little dirty boys,
You'll put your arms
Round her neck and love her.

To an Idealist

All that I scribble
Her eyes must see,
Who rends the body
And soul of me.

What might I scribble
If she weren't there?
Many a secret
Would I lay bare.

Then might she wonder
That love and hate,
Irreconcilable,
Yet can mate.

I think her selfish
And cold and hard, —
Give her black titles
That stretch a yard.

Yet in a minute
My breath is spent,
Swearing her noble
And innocent.

Must love be feeble
Where hate is set?
Loving or hating,
I can't forget.

'To Plato's dictum'

To Plato's dictum
Assent she lends.
All things in common
We hold, as friends.

I share her riches.
In days to be
She'll come and share in
My poverty.

'All day long'

All day long
We sew fine muslin up for you to wear,
Muslin that women wove for you elsewhere,
A million strong.

Just like flames,
Insatiable, you eat up all our hours
And sun and loves and tea and talk and flowers,
Suburban dames.

Ruffs for Hilda Esson

I'm making such pretty black ruffs
For thee to wear,
Oh white-faced lady with wide grey eyes
And bright red hair.

Up and down, with a buzz and a whirr,
My needle goes.
Shadow-soft as a creek in a dream
The dark tulle flows.

One day over the pleats and the folds
Thou'lt smile at me.
For are not these the prettiest ruffs
I make for thee?

'If you have loved a brave story'

If you have loved a brave story
Tell it but rarely;
And, with due faith in its glory,
Render it barely.

Then must the listener, hearing
Your tale of wonder,
Let his own hoping and fearing
Tear him asunder.

'O flame that bloweth with the wind'

O flame that bloweth with the wind
My flame thou art.
An all-enraptured glance I throw
In thy bright heart.

O blessing that the sun and wind
Have made thee strong,
Else hadst thou been by thy fierce soul
Consumed ere long.

'Once I could say pretty things'

Once I could say pretty things.
Can I not still?
Once I could with word and voice
Work all my will.
Once I could say pretty things
Can I not still?

Long I've languished lonely, love,
And could not speak.
Now thou'st come to make me strong
Who have been weak.
Long I've languished lonely, love,
But now can speak.

'You are more fair than shadows are'

You are more fair than shadows are
That toss and sway in windy aisles.
They have your grace, and Mystery,
But lack your smiles.

You are as fair as that slant sun
Whose blessing's on the moving trees,
And they who claim your friendship go
Arrayed like these.

'I dare not leave the splendid town'

I dare not leave the splendid town
To go where morning meadows are,
For somewhere here the Future's hid
In factory, shop, or liquor bar.

And when the picture shows are closed
She goes to roam about the docks.
Oh, she has wisdom on her mouth
And blood with honey in her locks.

I dare not read of Rosamund
Or such sweet ladyhood in books,
Lest dreaming on their excellence
I should forget the Future's looks.

And I'll walk lonely all my days
Down city pavements without end,
For with young love on flowery paths
I'd have small need of her to friend.

Yea, I would fain forget to sing,
Like larks in city prison bound,
In case I should not hear her voice
Above that clatter of sweet sound.

The Immigrant

When Gertie came in
To work today
She was much less weary
And far more gay.

We asked her the reason
Of this delight.
She had been dreaming
Of home all night.

'Child Sun'

Child Sun
Why will you play Peep Bo
Now in, now out,
The workroom window so?

True 'tis
That there are children here;
But they've no time
To play Peep Bo, my dear.

'Emmie, Emmie Adams'

Emmie, Emmie Adams,
With her insolent air,
Tied a little bit of rag
In her yellow hair.

When Lena, wondering,
Asked why it was there,
Emmie said she didn't know
And she didn't care.

I think Emmie Adams,
Though you are so fair,
That must be the devil's horn
In your yellow hair.

'Today when you went up the hill'

Today when you went up the hill
And all that I could see
Was just a speck of black and white
Very far from me,

It seemed more strange than words can say;
The dot that I could see
Really was the dearest thing
The world holds for me.

'Today I saw'

Today I saw
A market cart going along the road,
High-piled and creaking with a sonsy load
Of cabbages.

The driver sat
Under a little tent himself had made
To give him shelter from the rain or shade
In summertime.

Such men as he,
Backed by the riches of a countryside,
Should have kings' faces, full of jolly pride
In comeliness.

But he was tired
After a night's work under starlit skies,
And crouched like a poor slave, with anxious eyes
Turned citywards.

'Cherry plum blossom in an old tin jug'

Cherry plum blossom in and old tin jug, —
Oh, it is lovely, beautiful and fair,
With sun on it and little shadows mixed
All in among the fragrant wonder there.

Cherry plum blossom on the workroom bench
Where we can see it all our working hours.
In all my garden days of ladyhood,
I never met girls who so loved sweet flowers.

'Each morning I pass on my way to work'

Each morning I pass on my way to work
A clock in a Tower
And I look towards it with anxious eyes
To make sure of the hour.

But the sun gets up at the back of the tower
With a flare and a blaze
Hiding the time and the tower from my sight
In a blissful haze.

"I am the marker of time," says the sun.
Taken unawares,
I believe for the nonce he is lord of the day
And am rid of my cares.

'I'd love to have you on a rainy day'

I'd love to have you on a rainy day
Tucked in a chair, my head against your knee
To sit and dream with. Sometime you must be
My home-sharer whom rain can't keep away.

'Sitting here daylong'

Sitting here daylong
I dream of you.
Sitting here daylong,
Sitting here daylong.

When the girls will talk
They break my dreams,
Sitting here daylong,
Sitting here daylong.

'Green and blue'

Green and blue
First-named of colours believe these two.
They first of colours by men were seen
This grass colour, tree colour,
Sky colour, sea colour,
Magic-named, mystic-souled, blue and green.

Later came
Small subtle colours like tongues of flame,
Small jewel colours for treasure trove,
Not fruit colour, flower colour,
Cloud colour, shower colour,
But purple, amethyst, violet and mauve.

These remain,
Two broad fair colours for our larger gain
Stretched underfoot or spreading wide on high,
Green beech colour, vine colour,
Gum colour, pine colour,
Blue of the noonday and the moonlit sky.

Fatherless

I've had no man
To guard and shelter me,
Guide and instruct me
From mine infancy.

No lord of earth
To show me day by day
What things a girl should do
And what she should say.

I have gone free
Of manly excellence
And hold their wisdom
More than half pretence.

For since no male
Has ruled me or has fed,
I think my own thoughts
In my woman's head.

Work-girl's Holiday

A lady has a thousand ways
Of doing nothing all her days,
And so she thinks that they're well spent;
She can be idle and content.
But when I have a holiday
I have forgotten how to play.

I could rest idly under trees
When there's some sun and little breeze
Or if the wind should prove too strong
Could lie in bed the whole day long.
But any leisured girl would say
That that was waste of holiday.

Perhaps if I had weeks to spend
In doing nothing without end,
I might learn better how to shirk
And never want to go to work.

Periodicity [I]

O shining moon,
Mother of months and of tides,
Over the women of Earth your rule abides.

We have our hours
Of dark, interlunar dream
Whence we emerge with bodies that shine and gleam
Like new-born flowers.

Is ocean weak
That changes, ebbs and returns?
Beauty in change is the beauty that cleanses, burns.
Though we may change,
Flicker and pause and glow,
Constant in beauty, strong from the crimson flow,
Through heaven we range.

Lawstudent and Coach

Each day I sit in an ill-lighted room
To teach a boy.
For one hour by the clock great words and dreams
Are our employ.

We read St Agnes' Eve and that more fair
Eve of St Mark
At a small table up against the wall
In the half-dark.

I tell him all the wise things I have read
Concerning Keats.
"His earlier work is overfull of sense
And sensual sweets."

I tell him all that comes into my mind
From God-knows-where,
Remark, "In English poets Bertha's type
Is jolly rare.

She's a real girl that strains her eyes to read
And cricks her neck.
Now Madeline could pray all night nor feel
Her body's check.

And Bertha *reads*, — p'rhaps the first reading girl
In English rhyme."
It's maddening work to say what Keats has said
A second time.

The boy sits sideways with averted head.
His brown cheek glows.
I like his black eyes and his sprawling limbs
And his short nose.

He, feeling, dreads the splendour of the verse,
But he must learn
To write about it neatly and to quote
These lines that burn.

He drapes his soul in my obscuring words,
Makes himself fit
To go into a sunny world and take
His part in it.

"Examiners' point of view, you know," say I,
"Is commonsense.
You must sift poetry before you can
Sift Evidence."

Periodicity [II]

Each month I go
Fathoms deep, ocean-whelmed, in woe.
Then agony, hopelessness roll
Wave-deep over body and soul,
Then pain's my familiar, darkness my friend,
And Time has no end.

Yet once again
I rise born anew from my pain.
Soul, body take radiant form.
Aphrodite-like out of the storm
I emerge. In their issue are blest
Those waves without rest.

Machinists Talking

I sit at my machine
Hourlong beside me, Vera, aged nineteen,
Babbles her sweet and innocent tale of sex.

Her boy, she hopes, will prove
Unlike his father in the act of love.
Twelve children are too many for her taste.

She looks sidelong, blue-eyed,
And tells a girlish story of a bride
With the sweet licence of Arabian queens.

Her child, she says, saw light
Minute for minute, nine months from the night
The mother first lay in her lover's arms.

She says a friend of hers
Is a man's mistress who gives jewels and furs
But will not have her soft limbs cased in stays.

I open my small store
And tell of a young delicate girl, a whore,
Stole from her mother many months ago.

Fate made the woman seem
To have a tiger's loveliness, to gleam
Strong and fantastic as a beast of prey.

I sit at my machine.
Hourlong beside me, Vera, aged nineteen,
Babbles her sweet and innocent tale of sex.

The Invisible People

When I go into town at half past seven
Great crowds of people stream across the ways,
Hurrying, although it's only half past seven.
They are the invisible people of the days.

When you go in to town about eleven
The hurrying, morning crowds are hid from view.
Shut in the silent buildings at eleven
They toil to make life meaningless for you.

Closing Time: Public Library

At ten o'clock the great gong sounds its dread
Prelude to splendour. I push back my chair,
And all the people leave their books. We flock,
Still acquiescent, down the marble stair
Into the dark where we can't read. And thought
Swoops down insatiate through the starry air.

The Two Swans

There's a big park just close to where we live, —
Trees in a row
And shaggy grass whereon the dead leaves blow.

And in the middle round a great lagoon
The fair yachts sail
In loveliness that makes the water pale.

Last night I went to walk along the road
Beside the park
And feel the kisses of the wintry dark.

It's the best place to watch the evening come,
For mists are there
And lights and shadows and the lake is fair.

And last night looking up I saw two swans
Fly overhead
With long black necks and their white wings outspread.

Above the houses citywards they went,
An arrowy pair
In secret, — white and black and dark and fair.

'Better than beauty's rose'

Better than beauty's rose
May be
A fair invisible word
As it flows
To me.

She has a lovely voice.
Oh hear
The little soft accents fall!
They rejoice
My ear.

Machinist's Song

The foot of my machine
Sails up and down
Upon the blue of this fine lady's gown.

Sail quickly, little boat,
With gifts for me, —
Night and the goldy streets and liberty.

'Up in my room on my unmade bed'

Up in my room on my unmade bed
I sat and read.

There was work waiting for me below.
I didn't go.

For in my little green room the song
Flickered along.

If the singer had seen the way it fared
She would have stared,

Have wondered and stared at me who read
With tumbled bed,

Wide-open window, wide-open door,
Books on the floor.

Hers was a disciplined, comely, wise
Christina-guise.

But what's the hell of a mess to me
When I am free

And wind blows in and a delicate song
Flickers along.

Body and Soul

Through the Museum
I stroll, and see
Goblets fashioned in Arcady,
Spears from the Islands, and robes from Tyre, —
Gew-gaws of pomp and of old desire.

On one of the walls
A looking glass
Catches my image as I pass.
Austerely from mirrored eyes, I see
The soul of the past look out at me.

"Our Vegetable Love"

It sprang in a night
From nothing at all
This love that it pleases me to call
This love that it teases you to call
A mushroom love.

But I know, I know
It will flourish long,
Nor in deserts languish. Fair and strong
It will grow in anguish. Fair and strong
As stately palms.

Periodicity [III]

My friend declares,
Being woman and virgin, she
Takes small account of periodicity

And she is right.
Her days are calmly spent
For her sex-function is irrelevant.

But I whose life
Is monthly broke in twain
Must seek some sort of meaning in my pain.

Women, I say,
Are beautiful in change,
Remote, immortal, like the moon they range.

Or call my pain
A skirmish in the whole
Tremendous conflict between body and soul.

Meaning must lie,
Some beauty surely dwell
In the fierce depths and uttermost pits of hell.

Yet still I seek,
Month after month in vain,
Meaning and beauty in recurrent pain.

'This evening I'm alone'

This evening I'm alone.
I wish there'd be
Someone to come along
And talk to me.

Yet out of all my friends
There isn't one
I'd like to come and talk
To me alone.

But if a stranger came
With newer brain
We'd yarn until we felt
Alive again.

'I was sad'

I was sad
Having signed up in a rebel band,
Having signed up to rid the land
Of a plague it had.

For I knew
That I would suffer, I would be lost,
Be bitter and foolish and tempest tost
And a failure too.

I was sad;
Though far in the future our light would shine,
For the present the dark was ours, was mine.
I couldn't be glad.

'They are so glad of a young companion'

They are so glad of a young companion,
They hail and bless me, these boys of mine,
And I whose pathway was dark and lonely
Have no more need for the sun to shine.

We'll walk in darkness, obscure, despised,
We'll mourn each other at prison gates.
These boys are splendid as mountain eagles
But mountain eagles have eagle mates.

The girls who prattle of work and pleasure,
Of last week's picnic and this week's joys,
Of past and present, nor heed the future,
Are lagging comrades for dawnstruck boys.

'I saw a flight of sparrows through the air'

I saw a flight of sparrows through the air.
Oh, let us rise
Out of the weaknesses of our despair
To burning skies.

Let us take wings for flight from home and friends
And sweet desire.
From comfortable earth the soul ascends
To heavens of fire.

'O little plum tree in the garden, you're'

O little plum tree in the garden, you're
Aflower again,
With memories of a million springs and my
Brief years of pain.

O little tree, you have the power to find
Your youth again.
Grow young, while I grow old in Tenderness
And wise in pain.

'The God who made this universe'

The God who made this universe
Gave various precepts to inspire.
"Remember, man, thou art but dust.
Thou hast no spark of sacred fire."

Man must be perfect as is God,
And like the lilies spurn desire.
"Remember, man, thou art but dust.
Thou hast no spark of sacred fire."

And man must love, man must forgive,
And hold the truth and never tire.
"Remember, man, thou art but dust.
Thou hast no spark of sacred fire."

Oh God is jealous, just, and cruel,
Yet still with man he may aspire.
"Remember, God, thou art not dust.
Thou hast thy spark of sacred fire."

'He has picked grapes in the sun. Oh, it seems'

He has picked grapes in the sun. Oh, it seems
Like a fairy tale,
Like a Tale of dreams.

"He in his slender youth, with vines, with sun,
Under a blazing sky", —
The tale might run.

There's beauty for eye and mind, for sight and thought,
Here on the surface.
Plunge. This beauty's nought.

Vision succeeds to dream. Deep in his heart
Fierier beauty lives
Than this surface art.

He has no song to sing of fragrant soil
Who in his heart revolts
At unlovely toil.

He has known the real, the truth of it. It seems
Misery eats the heart
Out of fairest dreams.

He in his slender youth, at strife, in vain
Offers his life to set
The world right again.

'The love I look for'

The love I look for
Could not come from you.
My mind is set to fall
At Peterloo.
But you'd protect me,
I'd be safe with you.

You could but love me
In the olden way, —
With gifts of jewels, children,
Time to play,
Be man to woman
In the olden way.

The love that's love has
Other gifts to bring, —
A share in weakness, dreams,
And suffering.
These are the only
Gifts I'd have to bring.

The love I look for
Does not come from you.
I see it dawning in
Deep eyes of blue.
I dare to hope for
Love, but not from you.

'He has a fairy wife'

He has a fairy wife.
He does not know her.
She is the heart of the storm,
Of the clouds that lower.

And as the clouds are torn
Into rain and thunder,
She in her brightness tears
His heart asunder.

'All through the day at my machine'

All through the day at my machine
There still keeps going
A strange little tune through heart and head
As I sit sewing:
    "There is a child in Hungary,
      A child I love in Hungary"
The words come flowing.

When I am walking home at night
That song comes after,
And under the trees in holiday time
Or hearing laughter:
    "I have a son in Hungary,
      My little son in Hungary"
Comes following after.

'Sometimes I wish that I were Helen-fair'

Sometimes I wish that I were Helen-fair
And wise as Pallas,
That I might have most royal gifts to pour
In love's sweet chalice.

Then I reflect my dear love is no god
But mortal only
And in this heavenly wife might deem himself
Not blest, but lonely.

'Sometimes I am too tired'

Sometimes I am too tired
To think of you.
Today was such a day,
But then I knew
Today, for certain, you'd be weary too.

You there in hospital
With health to seek, —
And me at my machine
Too tired to speak, —
We're very funny lovers of a week.

'My lovely pixie, my good companion'

My lovely pixie, my good companion,
You do not love me, bed-mate of mine,
Save as a child loves, —
Careless of loving,
Rather preferring raspberry wine.

How can you help it? You were abandoned.
Your mother left you. Your father died.
All your young years of
Pain and desertion
Are not forgotten, here at my side.

'Into old rhyme'

Into old rhyme
The new words come but shyly.
Here's a brave man
Who sings of commerce dryly.

Swift-gliding cars
Through town and country winging,
Like cigarettes,
Are deemed unfit for singing.

Into old rhyme
New words come tripping slowly.
Hail to the time
When they possess it wholly.

'Those must be masts of ships the gazer sees'

Those must be masts of ships the gazer sees
On through the little gap in the park trees
So far away that seeing almost fails.
Those must be masts, — the lovely masts of ships
Stripped bare of sails.

There's nothing here to please the seeing eyes, —
Four poles with crossway beams against the skies.
But beauty's not for sight. True beauty sings
Of latent movement to the unsensed soul
In love with wings.

'I have golden shoes'

I have golden shoes
To make me fleet.
They are like the wind
Underneath my feet.

> When my lover's kiss
> Is overbold,
> I can run away
> In my shoes of gold.

Nay, when I am shod
With this bright fire,
I am forced to run
From my own desire.

> From the love I love
> Whose arms enfold
> I must run away
> In my shoes of gold.

'Now I've been three days'

Now I've been three days
In the place where I am staying,
I've taken up new ways, —
Landowning and flute playing.

There's an orchard ground
Seen, that set me sighing.
Should I give ten pounds,
It is mine for buying.

With the door set wide
I could sit there playing,
Send the magic notes
Through the gully straying.

Since the roof is sound
And the trees are growing,
I will give ten pounds,
All my gold bestowing.

Now I've been three days
In the place where I am staying,
I've taken up new ways, —
Landowning and flute playing.

'I found an orchid in the valley fair'

I found an orchid in the valley fair,
And named it for us both,
And left it there.

Two flowers upon one stem, white-souled, alone, —
I couldn't pull them up,
And bring them home.

A Bad Snap

He: That isn't you.
She: It's me, in my blue skirt
    And scarlet coat and little golden shoes.
He: Not good enough.
She: Well, burn it if you choose
    And take myself.
He: Yourself like skies and days
    To praise and live in, worship and abuse.

'You may have other loves'

You may have other loves, —
Red mouths to kiss.
Why should you lose
That loveliness for this?

No loveliness of mine
That comes and goes
Wild-fuchsia-like
Need blind you to the rose.

So I, who bless
Your hot and passionate ways,
Still need the starry loves
Of virgin days.

'Oh, but September is the month of flowers'

Oh, but September is the month of flowers
Right month to welcome this beloved of ours
This darling blossom on maternal hills
Born with the poppies and the daffodils.

Th' Inconstant Moon

The young moon at evening
Hides in a cloud
A pale moon
A fair moon
Wrapped in her shroud.

But when the night falls
She will come out
A full moon
A true moon
Fair love to flout.

The Contest

Our palm designed to grow
In deserts, sent roots seeking far and wide
Channels where waters flow.

And in the city found
Intricate pipings where the waters flow
Imprisoned underground.

Since iron strength was nought
Against the clever groping fingers, meant
To find the thing they sought,

Our palm's condemned to go;
While on through streets and houses at men's will
Rivers of crystal flow.

Be sad awhile. And then
Exult in visible beauty overthrown
By the fair will of men.

'Florence kneels down to say her prayers'

Florence kneels down to say her prayers
At night.
I wonder what she says and why she cares
To pray at night.

I think when she kneels down to pray
At night
The names that have been on her lips all day
Are there, at night.

She interferes with destinies
At night.
My loves are free to do the things they please
By day, or night.

'I love to see'

I love to see
Her looking up at me,
Stretched on a bed
In her pink dressing gown,
Her arms above her head,
Her hair all down.
I love to see
Her smiling up at me.

'O man, O woman, grievest so?'

O man, O woman, grievest so?
Art shut away from all delight,
And must thou leave this garden plot?
O Eve, O Adam, question not.
The God is kind who would be cruel.
He does not know the hearts he made.
Turn unreluctant to the shade,
To bitterest struggle, darkest night;
O man, O woman, happier so.

'Over your dear head'

Over your dear head
From day to day
The shadow minutes brood
And flit away.

In the darkened house
You dream through life,
An insubstantial ghost
Debarred from strife.

Dear you are, my dear,
And young and fair,
Dream-fettered in your home,
Imprisoned there.

'She has all Ireland in her blood'

She has all Ireland in her blood, —
All Ireland's need of sword and tears,
With memories dim before the flood,
And conflicts of a thousand years.

No son of Italy should love
A heart the centuries have worn.
She had no thought of kissing lips,
She held her womanhood in scorn.

And all her joy is blackest pain,
And all her love is bitter woe.
Then you must leave her side again.
That is no path for you to go.

The Melbourne Cup

I like the riders
Clad in rose and blue,
Their colours glitter
And their horses too.

Swift go the riders
On incarnate speed.
My thought can scarcely
Follow where they lead.

Delicate, strong, long
Lines of colour flow,
And all the people
Tremble as they go.

'There is a child's name that I want to say'

There is a child's name that I want to say
Though the child lives ten thousand miles away
And I've no notion what his name may be.
It is some strange wild word of Hungary.

And I've no way of knowing if he brooks
To bear his father's image in his looks.
But he is beautiful. There's none above him.
He is my lover's son and so I love him.

The Nuns and the Lilies

The lilies in the garden walk
Are out today.
The nuns all came to look at them,
To look and say
They wouldn't last to deck the crib
On Christmas day.

They had outstripped the Holy Child.
And yet at least
They should have been for Ursula,
Lucy, Joan, Perpetua, —
Have glittered on the altar through some virgin feast.

The lilies in the convent walk
Are fair to see.
They have forgotten baby Christs,
It seems to me.
They laugh and toss their royal heads
In ecstasy.

And still they say I must believe
Like princely churls
For all your lovely purity,
Catherine, Mary, Dorothy,
We will not die as altar flowers for dreaming girls.

'I have no force to hold my love'

I have no force to hold my love,
No loveliness to keep him by.
I am so weary of my life
I wish to die.

If I lie down and never eat
And hardly speak or draw my breath
I'll fall asleep and dream and fall
From sleep to death.

'I am afraid'

I am afraid
He'll someday stop loving me.
All of them say
He'll someday stop loving me, —
That's how he's made.

If I upbraid
And say he'll stop loving me
He always swears
He'll never stop loving me.
But I'm afraid.

'I'm like all lovers, wanting love to be'

I'm like all lovers, wanting love to be
A very mighty thing for you and me.

In certain moods your love should be a fire
That burnt your very life up in desire.

The only kind of love then to my mind
Would make you kiss my shadow on the blind

And walk seven miles each night to see it there,
Myself within, serene and unaware.

But you're as bad. You'd have me watch the clock
And count your coming while I mend your sock.

You'd have my mind devoted day and night
To you and care for you and your delight.

Poor fools, who each would have the other give
What spirit must withhold if it would live.

You're not my slave, I wish you not to be.
I love yourself and not your love for me,

The self that goes Ten thousand miles away
And loses thought of me for many a day.

And you loved me for loving much beside
But now you want a woman for your bride.

Oh, make no woman of me, you who can,
Or I will make a husband of a man.

By my unwomanly love that sets you free
Love all myself, but least the woman in me.

'I used to be afraid to meet'

I used to be afraid to meet
The lovers going down our street.

I'd try to shrink to half my size
And blink and turn away my eyes.

But now I'm one of them I know
I never need have bothered so.

And they won't mind it if I stare
Because they'll never know I'm there.

Or if they do, they're proud to be
Fond lovers for the world to see.

'I love a little boy'

I love a little boy
Who lives so far away.
If only he were here
I'd kiss him every day.

He should be brushed and dressed
And spoiled as kiddies are.
If only he were near
Whom fate has set so far.

Buddha in the Workroom

Sometimes the skirts I push through my machine
Spread circlewise, strong-petalled lobe on lobe,
And look for the rapt moment of a dream
Like Buddha's robe.

And I, caught up out of the workroom's stir
Into the silence of a different scheme,
Dream, in a sun-dark, templed otherwhere,
His alien dream.

Skirt Machinist

I am making great big skirts
For great big women, —
Amazons who've fed and slept
Themselves inhuman.

Such long skirts, not less than two
And forty inches.
Thirty round the waist for fear
The webbing pinches.

There must be tremendous tucks
On those round bellies.
Underneath, the limbs will shake
Like wine-soft jellies.

I am making such big skirts
And all so heavy,
I can see their wearers at
A lord-mayor's levee.

I who am so small and weak
I've hardly grown
Wish the skirts I'm making less
Unlike my own.

Dilectus meus

O my most precious fair one
Elect are you,
Preferred above the others, —
I tell you true.

But I had many lovers
When I was young
Who have not passed forgotten,
Their names unsung.

I would not wish to tell you
Or wish 'twere true
That I'd had many lovers
And loved but you.

'We climbed that hill'

We climbed that hill,
The road flushed red in pride
At being beauty's boundary. Either side
Stretched beauty, beauty ever, beauty still.

For on the left
Rose sandhills bound together by the deft
Long fingers of sea-grass,
Humped like the Punch and Judy of a farce,
Comical, cleft
With gaps for wind to pass,
Spotted
With dark
Clumped tea-tree, stark
With rushes, fierce with burrs,
Blotted
With purple earth,
Stains, remnants, marks of birth
On too-exuberant beauty.

On the right
Long paddocks stooped under a cloudy sky.

"They're lovely paddocks. Look at them," you said.
I turned my head.
What I'd thought gray
Was seen
To be the young beginning of live green
Under a spray
Of ghostly weed-stalks, — lilacs, mauves and blues

At interplay, —
A delicate tracery of shadow hues.

"There's colour", — I began,
And straightway knew
I saw what you
Saw not, and yet your vision was not mine.
Your eyes were on the line,
The sweep and curve of the fields against the sky.
You'd heard
My poor beginning of a word.
I had no more to praise
An unfamiliar loveliness. To gaze
Was all my praise.

At the hilltop it was your turn to say
"There's colour." You had found
Silver and gold on my Tom Tiddler's ground.
At the roadside
A clump of grasses, all
Caught round a little bush and tangled, tied
With unimagined colours people call
Green when they see them. This was treasure spied
By your eyes with my soul.
You'd liked the whole
Broad sweep of things, had scarcely seen such small
Jewel incidents until
I showed you, who had never watched a hill
Remote in contemplation 'neath far, far skies
Except with eyes
That had no mind to see
A present beauty, — only what might be
If distance were annihilate.

And then,
Where the road crossed the creek we could not cross,
We found again
Our power of sight redoubled by the loss

Of what I'd planned.
You said it was no sense
To pull off shoes and fasten up a skirt
And plunge through dirt
And mud
And water, — water
Muddy,
Ruddy,
As zinnias and paint-water and a flood
Of heavy auburn hair. We'd better go
Round by the beach,
Not by the cliffs, to reach
That farthest cliff I wanted to see tower
Above the waves in colour and in power, —
More solid than the sky.

And so
We turned
Seaward among the sea-grass. I had learned
Some of your alien sense of beauty, line
Preferred to colour, distance to the near.
For it was I
Who saw
The lovely curve of the creek.
But the whole shore
Yellow, untrodden, (more
The loveliest thing of our whole lovely week
For subtle curve, unbroken surface, than
For colour) this wide shore
Was yours and mine
And yours and mine the foam
When it would shine
Flower-coloured in a glint of sun. But mine
The hurry
And swift scurry
Of wind-blown tea-tree up the cliff.

We gave
A double dower
Of beauty to each wave
That trailed its hair in the wind before it broke.
For all the power
Of alien philosophies awoke
Our power of sight.
You still proclaim the far
Eternal unity of things that are
Like Plato and the mountains. I prefer
Inchoate beauty, for my part aver
Plurality essential, am content
To find a gain in difference, — in a while
Admit there's gain in union. Argument
Recurs. Oh well, at any rate we know
That walk was lovely; —
Ecstasies of mind
And subtle mysteries of sight combined
With the dear love of friends to make it so.

'I have to make a soul for one'

I have to make a soul for one
Who lost his soul in childhood's hour.
And I'm not sure, — not really sure, —
If I have power.

I don't know whether souls are made
With laughter or with faith or pain
But though I fail a thousand times
I'll try again.

'Under the pier'

Under the pier
By the darkened sea
Palamon told
A dream to me, —

A dream of the sky
With Venus there
No other star
In the midnight air,

But only Venus
Blessing the sea
Fashioning gold
From ebony.

To the golden waves
A maiden came
And opened her heart
For Venus' flame.

Under the pier
By the darkened sea
Palamon told
This dream to me.

A Blouse Machinist

Miss Murphy has blue eyes and blue-black hair,
Her machine's opposite mine
So I can stare
At her pale face and shining blue-black hair.

I'm sure that other people think her plain
But I could look at her
And look again
Although I see why people think her plain.

She's nice to watch when her machine-belt breaks.
She has such delicate hands
And arms, it takes
Ages for her to mend it when it breaks.

Oh, beauty's still elusive and she's fine.
Though all the moulding
Of her face, — the line
Of nose, mouth, chin, — is Mongol, yet she's fine.

Of course things would be different in Japan.
They'd see her beauty.
On a silken fan
They'd paint her for a princess in Japan.

But still her loveliness eludes the blind.
They never use their eyes
But just their mind.
So must much loveliness elude the blind.

An Improver

Maisie's been holding down her head all day,
Her little red head. And her pointed chin
Rests on her neck that slips so softly in
The square-cut low-necked darling dress she made
In such a way, since it's high-waisted too,
It lets you guess how fair young breasts begin
Under the gentle pleasant folds of blue.

But on the roof at lunchtime when the sun
Shone warmly and the wind was blowing free
She lifted up her head to let me see
A little rosy mark beneath her chin, —
The mark of kisses. If her mother knew
She'd be ashamed, but a girl-friend like me
Made her feel proud to show her kisses to.

Mortal Poems

I think each year should bring
Little fresh songs
Like flowers in spring

That they might deck the hours
For a brief while
And die like flowers.

Flower-like content to be
Sharers in man's
Mortality.

Beauty and Terror

Beauty does not walk through lovely days.
Beauty walks with horror in her hair.
Down long centuries of pleasant ways
Men have found the terrible most fair.

Youth is lovelier in death than life,
Beauty's mightier in pain than joy.
Doubly splendid burn the fires of strife,
Brighter in the brightness they destroy.

Grotesque

My
Man
Says
I weigh about four ounces,
Says I must have hollow legs.
And then say I,
"Yes,
I've hollow legs and a hollow soul and body.
There is nothing left of me.
You've burnt me dry.

You
Have
Run
Through all my veins in fever,
Through my soul in fever for
An endless time.
Why,
This small body is like an empty snail shell,
All the living soul of it
Burnt out in lime."

Beauty's Fires

She is not of the fireside,
My lovely love,
Nor books, nor ev'n a cradle,
She bends above.

No, she is bent with lashes,
Her flesh is torn.
From blackness into blackness
She walks forlorn.

Till round her captive body
The flames are bright
Because they feed on beauty
And flare through night.

Oh beauty is not beauty
Except in strife.
Hers are the fires of conflict
Twixt death and life.

'This is a pretty road'

This is a pretty road
With lamps a-swinging
And all along the way
Motor cars winging.

There are wires overhead
Like webs of spiders
And underneath them go
A million riders.

Under this tracery
Where trams go speeding
Seaward or cityward
The road is leading.

'Once I thought my love was worth the name'

Once I thought my love was worth the name
If tears came.

When the wound is mortal, now I know,
Few tears flow.

'You want a lily'

You want a lily
And you plead with me
"Give me my lily back."

I went to see
A friend last night and on her mantelshelf
I saw some lilies,
Image of myself,
And most unlike your dream of purity.

They had been small green lilies, never white
For man's delight
In their most blissful hours.
But now the flowers
Had shrivelled and instead
Shone spikes of seeds,
Burned spikes of seeds,
Burned red
As love and death and fierce futurity.

There's this much of the lily left in me.

'Tonight when woes are manifold'

Tonight when woes are manifold
I count the fingers of this land
And all its hollows, — understand
How little bliss such hands may hold.

For Lavender and Neutral Bay
And all the points of black and gold,
Though they are lovely to behold
And star-bedecked and warm and gay,

Are not like hands I used to kiss
Dear fragile human hands of clay, —
And I'll not clasp for many a day
Those hands that hold my all of bliss.

'Pink eucalyptus flowers'

Pink eucalyptus flowers
(The flowers are out)
Are scented honey sweet
For bees to buzz about.

Pink eucalyptus flowers
(The flowers are out)
Are fair as any rose
For us to sing about.

Rebels

All the girls in the park
Underneath such tender skies
Make the workday city seem
Very lovely in our eyes.

But although stars and lights
Fall so softly on the grass,
Our desire is fixed to see
The rebellion come to pass.

'I came to live in Sophia Street'

I came to live in Sophia Street,
In a little house in Sophia Street,
With an inch of floor
Between door and door
And a yard you'd measure in children's feet.

When I'd been ten days in Sophia Street
I remembered its name was Wisdom Street;
For I'd learned much more
Than in all the score
Of the years I clamoured for books to eat.

'Every night I hurry home to see'

Every night I hurry home to see
If a letter's there from you to me.

Every night I bow my head and say,
"There's no word at all from him today."

A Scrapheap

He whom I love was first to love me;
He whom I love I know is true;
And the sky can never be gray above me,
Or birds stop singing the whole year through.

Matters like space and time are stupid, —
Limits outgrown the heart knows how.
And we've done forever with teasing Cupid.
A fairer deity rules us now.

'I thought I heard something move in the house'

I thought I heard something move in the house
When I was alone in bed.
And I was afraid … and I was afraid …
I lay, — I quaked for dread.

Then all of a sudden the rain began
And I knew that the sound I'd heard
Was only the sound of the coming of rain.
Me, I've the heart of a bird!

'Today is rebels' day. And yet we work'

Today is rebels' day. And yet we work,
All of us rebels, until day is done.
And when the stars come out we celebrate
A revolution that's not yet begun.

Today is rebels' day. And men in jail
Tread the old mill-round until day is done.
And when night falls they sit alone to brood
On revolution that's not yet begun.

Today is rebels' day. Let all of us
Take courage to fight on until we're done, —
Fight though we may not live to see the hour
The Revolution's splendidly begun.
May Day, 1918

'To look across at Moira gives me pleasure'

To look across at Moira gives me pleasure.
She has a red tape measure.

Her dress is black and all the workroom's dreary,
And I am weary.

But that's like blood, — like a thin blood stream trickling, —
Like a fire quickening.

It's Revolution. *Ohé*, I take pleasure
In Moira's red tape measure.

Street Music

There's a band in the street, there's a band in the street,
It will play you a tune for a penny, —
It will play you a tune, you a tune, you a tune,
And you, though you haven't got any.

For the music's free, and the music's bold.
It cannot really be bought and sold.

And the people walk with their heads held high
Whether or not they've a penny.
And the music's there as the bandsmen know,
For the poor, though the poor are many.

Oh the music's free and the music's bold.
It cannot really be bought and sold.

'I dreamt last night of happy home-comings'

I dreamt last night of happy home-comings.
Friends I had loved and had believed were dead
Came happily to visit me and said
I was a part of their fair home-coming.

It's strange that I should dream of welcomings
And happy meetings when my love, last week
Returned from exile, did not even speak
Or write to me or need my welcoming.

'He looks in my heart and the image there'

He looks in my heart and the image there
Is himself, himself, than himself more fair.

And he thinks of my heart as a mirror clear
To reflect the image I hold most dear.

But my heart is much more like a stream, I think,
Where my lover may come when he needs to drink.

And my heart is a stream that seems asleep
But the tranquil waters run strong and deep;

They reflect the image that seems most fair
But their meaning and purpose are otherwhere.

He may come, my lover, and lie on the brink
And gaze at his image and smile and drink

While the hidden waters run strong and free,
Unheeded, unguessed at, the soul of me.

'My window pane is broken'

My window pane is broken
Just a bit
Where the small curtain doesn't
Cover it.

And in the afternoon
I like to lie
And watch the pepper tree
Against the sky.

Pink berries and blue sky
And leaves and sun
Are very fair to rest
One's eyes upon.

And my tired feet are resting
On the bed
And there's a pillow under
My tired head.

Parties and balls and books
I know are best
But when I've finished work
I like to rest.

'Sometimes I think the happiest of love's moments'

Sometimes I think the happiest of love's moments
Is the blest moment of release from loving.

The world once more is all one's own to model
Upon one's own and not another's pattern.

And each poor heart imprisoned by the other's
Is suddenly set free for splendid action.

For no two lovers are a single person
And lovers' union means a soul's suppression.

Oh, happy then the moment of love's passing
When those strong souls we sought to slay recover.

'O sweet and fair! These words are mine to use'

O sweet and fair! These words are mine to use.
O sweet and fair! A year ago I'd choose
Some better words of praise
Than sweet and fair.

O sweet and fair, and weak, and most untrue!
O sweet and fair! I still may speak of you
After my year of pain
As sweet and fair.

'The people have drunk the wine of peace'

The people have drunk the wine of peace
In the streets of town.
They smile as they drift with hearts at rest
Uphill and down.

The people have drunk the wine of peace,
They are mad with joy.
Never again need they lie and fear
Death for a boy.

Girl's Love

I lie in the dark
Grass beneath and you above me,
Curved like the sky,
Insistent that you love me.

But the high stars
Admonish to refuse you
And I'm for the stars
Though in the stars I lose you.

'I went down to post a letter'

I went down to post a letter
Through the garden, through the garden.
All the lovely stars were shining
As I went.
They were free as I, unhappy
Only he to whom the letter
Must be sent.

Even stars forget the prisons,
Stars and clouds and moonlit waters.
I believe the wind would shun them
If it could.
He at least rebels, — remembers
Dawn breaks eastward, where the prisons
Erstwhile stood.

'I must be dreaming through the days'

I must be dreaming through the days
And see the world with childish eyes
If I'd go singing all my life
And my songs be wise

And in the kitchen or the house
Must wonder at the sights I see.
And I must hear the throb and hum
That moves to song in factory.

So much in life remains unsung,
And so much more than love is sweet.
I'd like a song of kitchenmaids
With steady fingers and swift feet.

And I could sing about the rest
That breaks upon a woman's day
When dinner's over and she lies
Upon her bed to dream and pray

Until the children come from school
And all her evening work begins.
There's more in life than tragic love
And all the storied, splendid sins.

Slayers of Love

This girl who writes of love and broken hearts
Is young and wise.
She loves and dreams and looks at her beloved
With seeing eyes.

She thinks him blind and callous since he set
A jewelled bowl
Higher than all her diamond mystery
Of limbs and soul.

She states that yesterday he broke her heart, —
Oh, to my mind,
If he can deal a blow so swift and sure,
He must be kind.

'When I get up to light the fire'

When I get up to light the fire,
And dress with all the speed I may
By candle-light, I dread the hours
That go to make a single day.

But then I leave my room, and see
How brightly, clearly darkness shines,
When stars ten thousand miles away
Are caught in our verandah vines.

And I am almost glad that fires
Have to be lit, before the day
Comes up between the trees and drives
The strange familiar dark away.

'Today, in class'

Today, in class,
I read aloud to forty little boys
The legend of King Croesus' boasted joys.

They were so young,
Restless, and eager, I believed they'd find
This moral story little to their mind.

But they were pleased
With the old legend, — quick to comprehend
Sorrowful wisdom's triumph at the end:

They seemed to feel,
In hush of wonder, hurry of amaze,
The sure uncertainty of all men's days.

'One day she put two arms around me'

One day she put two arms around me, —
Two arms around, —
This splendid teacher whom I worship.
For a space I found

That, as she bent to mark my lesson
Down from above,
My head might rest in lover fashion
On the breast of love.

'I bought a red hat'

I bought a red hat
To please my lover.
He will hardly see it
When he looks me over,

Though it's a fine hat.
Yet he never misses
Noticing my red mouth
When it's shaped for kisses.

Miss Mary Fairfax

Every day Miss Mary goes her rounds
Through the splendid house and through the grounds, —

Looking if the kitchen table's white, —
Seeing that the great big fire's alight, —

Finding specks on shining pans and pots, —
Never praising much, and scolding lots.

If the table's white, she does not see
Roughened hands that once were ivory.

It is fires, not cheeks, that ought to glow;
And if eyes are dim, she doesn't know.

Blind Miss Mary! Poor for all she owns,
Since the things she loves are stocks and stones.

'Whenever I think of you, you are alone'

Whenever I think of you, you are alone, —
Shut by yourself between
Great walls of stone.

There is a stool, I think, and a table there,
And a mat underneath your feet;
And the rest is bare.

I cannot stop from remembering this, my own,
Seventeen hours of the day
You are alone.

A Strike Rhyme

The strike's done.
The men won.
The ships sail the sea
To bring back
What we lack, —
Coal, Sugar, Tea.

And I'm glad,
Though I had
Rather never use
Tea and spice
And what's nice
Than see the men lose.

'In this little school'

In this little school
Life goes so sweetly,
Day on azure day
Is lost completely.

No one thinks too much
Or worries greatly.
In a pleasant shade
We dream sedately.

There's no struggle here
Or conflict showing;
Only the sweet pain
Of young limbs growing.

'A lady and I were walking'

A lady and I were walking
Where waters flow;
A lady and I were talking
Softly and slow.

This is what you were saying,
Lady of mine,
"I will be sad without him,
Yea, I will pine.

But he would never leave me
If he were free.
That's what my love in prison
Whispered to me."

Three Teachers

Sometimes I can see
When I teach
Half my children talk
Each to each.

Then I almost wish
I could be
Very fierce and they
Scared of me.

They will all be still
For one man
Who could never teach
As I can.

He is kind and strong,
Narrow-souled.
He has never sought
Dangerous gold.

If he might do both
That were good.
In my life I knew
One who could.

She was dark and sweet,
Irish born,
Very full of dreams,
Full of scorn.

Hell and heav'n was she,
Like the sun.
My dear children need
Such a one.

'Now all the lovely days are past'

Now all the lovely days are past, —
The hours of sun, and leagues of sea,
And starry nights that lay between
Yourself and me.

Our boat has left the sea behind.
She lies beside the friendly dock.
And soon the gangway will go down,
And lips will meet, and hands will lock,

And carriers will come climbing up
To take my things, and leave us free.
There's trams and streets and home at last
For you and me.

Inventory

We've a room
That we call home,
With a bed in it,
And a table
And some chairs,
A to Z in it.
There's a mirror,
And a safe,
And a lamp in it.
Were there more,
Our mighty love
Might get cramp in it.

At Woolongong!

Oh, Bob, do you remember
I lay upon the beach there last September,
And thought of you in jail?
At Woolongong.

At Woolongong!
Later I wouldn't go there
In case I might miss seeing you. And to there
You are now free yourself,
At Woolongong.

One Man's Meat

The rain drifts down.
And the crops in the country grow.
And thousands of city workers
Lounge in a row
And curse and wait for the sun
To come out again.
Their work and their pay
Have been brought to an end
By the rain.

Shop Keeper and Customer

There was a great lady
Stamping on the floor.
I ran up the kitchen stair
And hurried to the door.

"You have kept me waiting,
How can this thing be?"
Why should a great lady
Frighten little me?

"If I've kept you waiting
I don't greatly care."
Out goes my great lady
With a haughty stare.

For this poor great lady
Doesn't like the truth.
She has never heard it
Since her distant youth.

A Parlourmaid

"I want a parlourmaid."
                "Well, let me see,
If you were God, what kind of maid she'd be."

"She would be tall,
 She would be fair,
 She would have slender limbs,
 A delicate air;
 And yet for all her beauty
 She would walk
 Among my guests unseen
 And through their talk
 Her voice would be the sweet voice of a bird,
 Not listened to, though heard."

"And now I know the girl you have in mind
 Tell me her duties, if you'd be so kind."
"Why, yes!
 She must know names of wines
 And never taste them, —
 Must handle fragile cups
 And never break them, —
 Must fill my rooms with flowers

And never wear them, —
Must serve my daughter's secrets
And not share them."

"Madam, you are no God, that's plain to see.
I'll just repeat what you have said to me.

You say your maid must look in Helen fashion
Golden and white
And yet her loveliness inspire no passion,
Give no delight.

Your intimate goods of home must owe their beauty
To this girl's care
But she'll not overstep her path of duty
Nor seek to share

Through loving or enjoying or possessing
The least of them.
    Why, she's not human, by your own confessing,
And you condemn

Your rational self in every word you're speaking!
Please understand
You'll find the hollow maiden you are seeking
In fairyland."

'When I go up to work the young blue sea'

When I go up to work the young blue sea
Has not awaked from dreams:
It fades to meet the blue sky mistily,
It gleams.
I say,
"All day
It will not wake from dreams."

And yet, when I come back from work, the sea
Has a green sombreness;
As if the hours between were somehow hours
Of stress.
I read
Its need
Of dim forgetfulness.

'I used to have dozens of handkerchiefs'

"I used to have dozens of handkerchiefs
Of finest lawn.
I used to have silk shirts and fine new suits", —
He's like a faun

This darling out-at-elbows Irish boy.
"Those were the days
Before the war
When money could be earned a thousand ways.

But now, — last week I had a muslin bag
For handkerchief!
No socks, no shirts", — but wiles and smiles and gleams
Beyond belief.

Learning Geography

They have a few little hours
To study the world, —
Its lovely absence of clouds,
Or the thunderbolts hurled
By hidden powers, —

All the soft shapes of the vales
And the trees of the north
They dream of a minute, no longer,
No longer, — then forth
Ere the year fails

To cities where carnival glows
Or the furnace is bright.
So is measured or leisured
According as teachers dispose
Their cosmic delight.

To E.B.

You died when you had lived as many years
As I have, so
You died when you had shed as many tears,
For other woe.

For I had lovers versed in giving pain
To such as I.
Your lovers were the wind and driving rain
And midnight sky.

Yet though your sorrows had another source
Your splendours, too,
A year of exile and a daily cross
I share with you.

'I'd like to spend long hours at home'

I'd like to spend long hours at home
With a small child to bother me.
I'd take her out to see the shops
And fuss about my husband's tea.

Instead of this I spend my days
In noisy schoolrooms, harsh and bare.
Unloved am I, since people give
Too many children to my care.

G.B.

I have a lover fugitive, —
A child of pain
At war with love; by mutual love
Is freedom slain.

He would rejoice in alien souls
Remote as stars,
Souls whom freedom does not grieve,
Who need no bars.

'I want this thing and that'

I want this thing and that, —
A pudding-bowl, a saucepan,
And a hat
For Pat.

I note some grease, — or grime, —
A cobweb on the ceiling.
Where's the time
For rhyme?

This being wife
Is not Romance, not Hate, not
"Love to the knife"
But life.

Wind at Night

I have put out mine enemy,
The strong North wind, —
Have closed the window and made fast
The fluttering blind.

Yet I can hear him roam around
From door to door,
Trying to find an entering place
To torture more.

'I have put off myself awhile'

I have put off myself awhile
And lead another kind of life
Than that where dreams were quickly deeds, —
Now I am wife.

But since those days were blessèd days
I've a poor dream about the past.
I'll set it down in words. To words
I fall at last.

Lovers Parted [I]

Old tales of lovers oft I read
Whose love is slain by one harsh deed,
Or killed by change, or cooled by sin,
Their unforgiving gloried in.

But now I love, since I'm alive,
To love a mortal I contrive.
Human I am. God he is not.
Such imperfection is our lot,

That we have wronged each other. Yet
I pray that I may not forget
My love for him, — that his for me
Outlasts long years as faithfully.

'Most people have a way of making friends'

Most people have a way of making friends
That's very queer.
They don't choose whom they like, but anyone
In some way *near*.

The girl beside them on the factory bench,
The girl next door,
Does. If they move then they forget the friend
They had before.

I choose the friends who suit me (one I found
Shut up in jail), —
Some nuns, some clerks, — Anna whose beauty was
Frankly for sale.

Of course I cannot see them every day.
That's as Fate sends.
Blind Fate may choose my times for me, but not,
Oh not, my friends.

The Psychological Craze

I in the library,
Looking for books to read,
Pulled one out twice to see
If it fulfilled my need.

Butler had written this
Autobiography.
Which of the Butlers, then?
I opened it to see.

He's an old general
Mounted upon a horse.
Thinkers don't write their lives,
But soldiers can, of course.

They write: "The regiment
Was sent to Omdurman,
Where Gordon died. To catch
The Mahdi was our plan."

Later — "The bride wore white
And she had golden hair.
Four bridesmaids bore her train
Up to the altar where

His Grace of Birmingham", —
It's the old rigmarole,
Names, facts and dates, — no word
In this about the soul.

No dreams, no sin, no tears!
Only the body thrives.
Upon such worthless things
Great soldiers base their lives.

No wonder wars are fought.
Loss of such life is small, —
Life bound to space and time,
Not infinite at all.

Lovers Parted [II]

With the awakening of the memory of a forbidden action there is combined the awakening of the tendency to carry out the action.
　　　　　　　　　　　　Totem and Taboo, S. Freud

Old memories waken old desires
Infallibly. While we're alive
With eye or ear or sense at all,
Sometimes must love revive.

But we'll not think, when some stray gust
Relumes the flicker of desire,
That fuel of circumstance could make
A furnace of our fire.

The past is gone. We must believe
It has no power to change our lives.
Yet still our constant hearts rejoice
Because the past survives.

Appearances

I hated them when I was four years old,
The bright pink berries on the pepper-tree.
And now they seem quite beautiful to me.

My tower of dreams when I was four years old
Was such a tree. Its branches hid me well,
Although I so disliked the berries' smell.

I had my dreams when I was four years old …
But groundling now, who once could mount in air,
I judge the high-swung bright pink berries fair.

About Trees

Here, in the Eastern garden's galaxy,
Two song-familiar trees grow side by side:
Arbutus, myrtle; like a mystery
Of maid and bride.

So strong are they, so full of flower and leaf! —
Heine's pale maidens circle in their shade,
And long-forgotten Irish girls of grief
Have hither strayed.

O maiden-haunted trees of Hindustan,
By shadowy fingers are your branches stirred;
And melodies breathe through you softer than
A whispered word.

A Deity

Sometimes I think God has his days
For being friends.
He says: "Forgive my careless ways.
No one pretends
I'm always kind; but for today
Do let's be friends."

And grudgingly I make reply,
"Nice sort of friends.
I think it's time you had a try
To make amends
For things you've done; but after all
Suppose we're friends."

Martha

Sometimes I lose
My power of loving for an hour or two,
Then I misuse
My knowledge of friends' secrets to abuse
Them far more heartily than others do.

Then I forget
Their splendid selves, the victories they've won,
And only fret
Because they fail me, when my needs are set
Above the dreams they've fixed their hopes upon.

New Window, St John's Hawksburn

St John looks up to Christ in the great window
And Christ looks upward to the rose above,
And light streams through upon apostles kneeling, —
Victims of glory, sacrificed to love.

Down in the church the pews are out of order.
Workmen climb ladders, seem to risk their lives.
And now and then a party of churchwardens
Enter, accompanied by enquiring wives.

But to the artist, who is keen on colour, —
And to the churchfolk, who are rich in pride, —
And to the workmen, who must earn their living, —
Religion's the excuse. It's nought beside.

'I could not change the world at all'

I could not change the world at all
For all but one of millions there.
This one my love had power to save
From hell's despair.

I gave him home for loneliness
And leisure for degrading toil.
Most lovely was the soul that fate
Had sought to spoil.

Yet million others walk the streets
Unfriended, starving, soon to die.
Seed of the angels whom I love
Eternally.

'They sent me pictures of the saints'

They sent me pictures of the saints
For stained-glass windows. They'll be set
High up in church for all to see:
Mary and Margaret.

Secure in comradeship with God,
Gracious and steadfast, stand they there
Wrapped in long robes of sanctity;
Only their feet are bare.

Ideals at one with the Ideal.
New ciphers in the heavenly code.
Only their naked feet recall
The thorns upon the road.

"All Knowledge …"

I know more about flowers,
And Pat knows about ships.
"Schooner" and "barquentine"
Are words of note on his lips.

Even "schooner, barque-rigged"
Has meaning for him. And yet
I don't believe he knows
Heart's ease from mignonette.

And whenever the daffodils,
Like visiting golden dames,
Honour our humble flat,
He has to ask their names.

'How funny it would be if dreamy I'

How funny it would be if dreamy I
Should leave one book behind me when I die
And that a book of Law, — this silly thing
Just written for the money it will bring.
I do hope, when it's finished, I'll have time
For other books and better spurts of rhyme.

'Pat wasn't Pat last night at all'

Pat wasn't Pat last night at all.
He was the rain, —
The Spring, —
Young Dionysus, white and warm, —
Lilac and everything.

'A bunch of lilac and a storm of hail'

A bunch of lilac and a storm of hail
On the same afternoon! Indeed I know
Here in the South it always happens so,
That lilac is companioned by the gale.

I took some hailstones from the window sill
And swallowed them in a communion feast.
Their transitory joy is mine at least,
The lilac's loveliness escapes me still.

Mine are the storms of spring, but not the sweets.

The Changing Hills

Old poets talked
Of the "eternal hills"
And "bases of the mountains";
Oh, they walked
And counted steps
And measured dreams out so!
For, unlike these,
The hills I know
Go whirling to and fro
Behind the trees.
Mount Juliet, —
On Monday morning set
Above the rest, —
At noon or even,
Is with the blest
In heaven.
Not a wraith
Remains to haunt an earthly resting place.
And, lo!
Those golden trees, that strayed
So exquisitely near
An hour ago,
Have wandered off again,
To disappear
In far blue shade.
Panton Hills

'O you, dear trees, you have learned so much of beauty'

O you, dear trees, you have learned so much of beauty,
You must have studied this only the ages long!
Men have thought of God and laughter and duty.
And of love. And of song.

But you, dear trees, from your birth to your hour of dying,
Have cared for this one way only of being wise.
Lovely, lovely, lovely, the sapling sighing.
Lovely the dead tree lies.
Montrose

'Last night, in a dream, I felt the peculiar anguish'

Last night, in a dream, I felt the peculiar anguish
Known to me of old;
And there passed me, not much changed, my earliest lover,
Smiling, suffering, cold.

This morning, I lay with closed lids under the blankets,
Lest with night depart
The truthful dream which restored to me with my lover
My passionate heart.

White Sunshine

The sun's my fire.
Golden, from a magnificence of blue,
Should be its hue.

But woolly clouds,
Like boarding-house old ladies, come and sit
In front of it.

White sunshine, then,
That has the frosty glimmer of white hair,
Freezes the air.

They must forget, —
So self-absorbed are they, so very old, —
That I'll be cold.

'Charles Lamb blasts out his litany of names'

Charles Lamb blasts out his litany of names,
"Alice" and "Saxon Edith" and the rest.
Of all the names I ever heard, this one, —
"Lesbia Baracchi", — pleases me the best.

Flowers and Light

Flowers have uncountable ways of pretending to be
Not solid, but moonlight or sunlight or starlight with scent.
Primroses strive for the colour of sunshine on lawns
Dew-besprent.

Freesias are flames wherein light more than heat is desired,
As candles on altars burn amethyst, golden and white.
Wall-flowers are sun, streaked with shade. Periwinkles blue noon
At the height.

A Bronte Legend

They say she was a creature of the moor,
A lover of the angels, silence bound.
She sought no friendships. She was too remote,
Her sister Charlotte found.

I know she nursed her brother till he died,
Although she didn't like him; that she had
Housework and all the ironing to do,
Because her maids were bad.

And in the midst of it she wrote a book.
There could have been small leisure for the moor
Or wandering! She used to mend and sew,
The family was so poor.

Her brother died. But she died just as soon
As she had nursed dear Charlotte through the shock
Of Patrick's death. Contemplative? Well, well! —
No Simeon of the Rock!

Pruning Flowering Gums

One summer day, along the street,
Men pruned the gums
To make them neat.
The tender branches, white with flowers,
Lay in the sun
For hours and hours,
And every hour they grew more sweet, —
More honey-like;
Until the street
Smelt like a hive, withouten bees.
But still the gardeners
Lopped the trees.

Then came the children out of school,
Noisy and separate
As their rule
Of being is. The spangled trees
Gave them one heart:
Such power to please
Had all the flowering branches strown
Around for them
To make their own.
Then such a murmuring arose
As made the ears
Confirm the nose
And give the lie to eyes. For hours
Child bees hummed
In the honey flowers.

They gathered sprigs and armfuls. Some
Ran with their fragrant
Burdens home,
And still returned; and after them
Would drag great boughs.
Some stripped a stem
Of rosy flowers and played with these.
Never such love
Had earthly trees
As these young creatures gave. By night,
The treasured sprays
Of their delight
Were garnered every one. The street
Looked, as the council liked it, neat.

Polytheist

One comes to love the little saints,
As years go by.
One learns to love the little saints.
"Oh hear me sigh,
St Anthony,
Find this for me.
I wish you'd try."

There must be many garden gods
A gardener sees.
There'd have to be an orchard god.
"Divinities,
Take honour due.
The long year through
Protect these trees."

The Mother and the Holy Child
Are friends to me.
I pray, "I am my mother's child.
I trust you'll see
That days are bright
And all goes right
With her and me."

"Love is not love ..."

When I was still a child
I thought my love would be
Noble, truthful, brave,
And very kind to me.

Then, all the novels said
That if my lover prove
No such man as this
He had to forfeit love.

Now I know life holds
Harder tasks in store.
If my lover fail
I must love him more.

Should he prove unkind,
What am I, that he
Squander soul and strength
Smoothing life for me?

Weak or false or cruel,
Love must still be strong.
All my life I'll learn
How to love as long.

'I have a beautiful house'

I have a beautiful house
Like a snail's shell;
The notable part of me
Is the house where I dwell.

I couldn't be quite content
(Such a snail am I)
If I hadn't a house to bear
On my back till I die.

The Moonlit Room

I know a room that's dark in daytime hours;
No sunbeams light it,
Whether in months of gloom or months of flowers,
So people slight it.

Yet in the noon of each succeeding night
The moon shines in it,
Goldenly waking dreamers to delight
For a love's minute.

In a dream light, they sigh and burn and kiss
And fall to slumber
Deeply once more. Thus bliss is piled on bliss
In goodly number.

Praise first is giv'n to sunshine and to rooms
Sunbright, — with reason.
Yet a wise man should choose a moonlit room
In his blood's season.

'I hate work so'

I hate work so
That I have found a way
Of making one small task outlast the day.

I will not leave
The garden and the sun,
In spite of all the work that should be done.

So when I go
To really make my bed
I've made it ten times over in my head.

Then as for meals!
I think I'd rather be
A nervous wreck than make a cup of tea.

The fire's so low
It isn't any good, —
While I sit planning to put on some wood.

One thing is sure, —
I pity other drones,
God having made me such a lazy-bones.

The Sisters

They used to say
Our mother brought us up like hot-house flowers,
From day to day
Such wondrous cares were ours
Her love inspired.

In truth we grew
Strangely. Unsought, as priestesses might be.
The girls we knew
Found tenderness. But we
Were more desired.

No doubt at all,
Our spirits drew the secret souls of men.
They would recall
Old dreams through us; and then
Make dreams their choice.

Creatures of light,
Sun-darkened by the shining of her love,
We knew the plight
Of Sibyls, thus to prove
Th' incarnate Voice.

A Meaning Learnt

I'm not his wife. I am his paramour:
His wayside love, picked up in journeying:
Rose of the hedgerows: — fragrant, till he fling
Me down beside the ditch, a droopèd thing
Some country boy may stick into his hat.
A paramour has no more use than that.

The Wife

He's out of work!
I tell myself a change should mean a chance,
And he must look for changes to advance,
And he, of all men, really needs a jerk.

But I hate change.
I like my kitchen with its pans and pots
That shine like new although we've used them lots.
I wouldn't like a kitchen that was strange.

And it's not true
All changes are for better. Some are worse.
A man had rather work, though work's a curse,
Than mope at home with not a thing to do.

No surer thing
Than that he'll get another job. But soon!
Or else I'll have to change. This afternoon
Would be the time, before I sell my ring.

Raiment

I cannot be tricked out in lovely clothes
All times, all days.
My mind has moods of hating pearl and rose
And jewel-blaze.

Nor is the body worthily attired
Unless the soul
Has visibly to nobleness aspired
And self-control.

'There is no need of hurrying'

There is no need of hurrying.
In months when heart and soul are dumb
I quiver in action, plunge in thought.
Silent, — not numb.

I am no instrument, dedicate
To loveliness of sound or sight, —
No tool of purpose, business-bound, —
No satellite.

'When I am articled'

When I am articled
The Law decrees
I shall devote my time
To stating fees

And learning about Actions,
Suits and Courts.
Then Deeds and Briefs and Grants
Must fill my thoughts.

While if a naughty
Little verse should find
Its way into a corner
Of my mind

I must not tell the chap
For whom I work.
He pays the penalty
If I should shirk

And take to writing books
And verse instead
Of "hereinafter," "duly,"
"Viz," "the said."

'When my lover put the sea between us'

When my lover put the sea between us
And went wandering in Italy
My poor silly heart miscalled his journey, —
"Leaving me."

Towns of Spain and Italy he stayed in,
Each and all of them to me unknown;
How could he find pleasure being a lover,
Being alone!

I believed his absence had estranged us
And across the heart-dividing sea
Sent him word that I no longer loved him.
Foolish me!

Truly I was not as fair as Venice,
Noble as Siena, strange as Rome.
Certainly he loved Milan and Florence
More than home.

Came his answer after months of waiting
Echoing my letter, lie for lie.
Truth or lies I know not. Which unfaithful, —
He or I.

'I read a statement in a newspaper'

I read a statement in a newspaper
That Twentyman, the manufacturer,
Found it was cheaper to deliver goods
By horse and lorry than by motor-truck
Or motor-van. So he had sold his trucks
To purchase horses. He dismissed those men
Who had mechanics' minds to re-employ
Drivers of horses, friends of animals.
Then life grew stronger in me because life
Had triumphed in this case and would perhaps
Finally triumph over the machine.
Even such mean commercial victory
Being better than no victory at all.

'I have two loves to learn'

I have two loves to learn
The near love and the far love
The love of everyday
And the star love.

Nor dare I yet pronounce
That name compelling.
I-a-v-e-h, E-m-a-n-u-e-l.
I am still spelling.

Love Celestial

My fire burns as the sun burns:
No need of wind to fan the flame:
No need of fuel to feed the same:
So love burns.

My life has swung from day to night.
For where the sun shines, there is day:
But it's the same sun, hidden away,
That makes night.

'I am no mystic. All the ways of God'

I am no mystic. All the ways of God
Are dark to me.
I know not if he lived or if he died
In agony.

My every act has reference to man.
Some human need
Of this one, or of that, or of myself
Inspires the deed.

But when I hear the Angelus, I say
A Latin prayer
Hoping the dim incanted words may shine
Some way, somewhere.

Words and a will may work upon my mind
Till ethics turn
To that transcendent mystic love with which
The Seraphim burn.

'What were the good of stars if none looked on them'

What were the good of stars if none looked on them
But mariners, astronomers and such!
The sun and moon and stars were made for lovers.
I know that much.

A Prayer to Saint Rosa

When I am so worn out I cannot sleep
And yet I know I have to work next day
Or lose my job, I sometimes have recourse
To one long dead, who listens when I pray.

I ask Saint Rose of Lima for the sleep
She went without, three hundred years ago
When, lying on thorns and heaps of broken sherd,
She talked with God and made a heaven so.

Then speedily that most compassionate saint
Comes with her gift of deep oblivious hours, —
Treasured for centuries in nocturnal space
And heavy with the scent of Lima's flowers.

NOTES ON THE POEMS

p. 2 "Rather like an Amazon schooled by Athena" – From Chapter 32 of George Meredith's last novel, *The Amazing Marriage* (1895).

p. 22 Presumably Flavio Gioja, a fabled thirteenth-century Italian mariner, reputed to have had a role in developing the sailor's compass. He never, in fact, existed.

p. 37 Dante Gabriel Rossetti (1828–82) painted 'A Sea-Spell' in 1877. His sonnet of the same name dates from 1870.

p. 40 Hilda Esson (1886–1953), née Bull. Belonged to the Melbourne circle of Vance and Nettie Palmer. Active in the theatre and in public health. Married to the poet and dramatist Louis Esson. See Peter Fitzpatrick's *Pioneer Players: The Lives and Loves of Louis and Hilda Esson* (1995).

p. 84 'Beauty's Fires' – In an alternative version of this poem, entitled 'Revolution', the following stanza replaces stanzas three and four:

> But factories and prisons
> Are far more fair
> Than home or palace gardens
> If she is there.

p. 101 'At Woolongong!' [*sic*]. Bob Besant, a member of the Industrial Workers of the World and one of the so-called 'Sydney Twelve', jailed on charges of treason.

INDEX OF TITLES

A Bad Snap 66
A Blouse Machinist 81
A Bronte Legend 118
'A bunch of lilac and a storm of hail' 115
A Deity 112
A Grown Up Sister 4
A la bien-aimée 21
'A lady and I were walking' 98
A Meaning Learnt 124
A Parlourmaid 102
A Prayer to Saint Rosa 130
A Scrapheap 88
A Sophistical Argument 25
A Soul in Flight 19
A Strike Rhyme 97
'All day long' 40
"All Knowledge ..." 114
'All through the day at my machine' 61
'Ay, ay, ay, the lilies of the garden' 5
About Trees 111
Adventurers 8
After Rain 18
An Improver 82
Appearances 111
At Woolongong! 101
Beauty and Terror 83
Beauty's Fires 84
'Better than beauty's rose' 53
Birthday 19
'Blind eyes have I' 34
Body and Soul 55
Buddha in the Workroom 74
'Charles Lamb blasts out his litany of names' 118
'Cherry plum blossom in an old tin jug' 46
'Child Sun' 44
Closing Time: Public Library 52
'Coloured scraps of paper' 36
Day's End 23
'Dearest, dearest' 26
Deliverance Through Art 34

Development 27
Dilectus meus 75
'Each day' 14
'Each morning I pass on my way to work' 46
'Emmie, Emmie Adams' 44
'Every night I hurry home to see' 87
Fatherless 48
'Florence kneels down to say her prayers' 68
Flowers and Light 118
G.B. 106
Geisha 3
Girl's Love 93
God Speaks 13
'Green and blue' 47
Grotesque 83
Hecate's Due 35
'He has a fairy wife' 61
'He has picked grapes in the sun. Oh, it seems' 59
'He looks in my heart and the image there' 90
Hero Worship 3
'How are the hours employed I spend with you' 36
'How funny it would be if dreamy I' 115
'I am afraid' 72
'I am no mystic. All the ways of God' 129
'I bought a red hat' 96
'I came to live in Sophia Street' 87
'I can't feel the sunshine' 17
'I could not change the world at all' 113
'I count the days until I see you, dear' 10
'I dare not leave the splendid town' 42
'I do hate the folk I love' 37
'I dreamt last night' 1
'I dreamt last night of happy home-comings' 90
'I found an orchid in the valley fair' 65
'I hate work so' 123
'I have a beautiful house' 122
'I have golden shoes' 64
'I have no force to hold my love' 72

'I have put off myself awhile' 107
'I have three loves who are all most dear' 32
'I have to make a soul for one' 80
'I have two loves to learn' 128
'I have years still in which to grow' 32
'I love a little boy' 74
'I love to see' 68
'I must be dreaming through the days' 93
'I must haul up prettiness' 6
'I read a statement in a newspaper' 128
'I saw a flight of sparrows through the air' 58
'I thought I heard something move in the house' 88
'I used to be afraid to meet' 73
'I used to have dozens of handkerchiefs' 104
'I want this thing and that' 106
'I was sad' 57
'I went down to post a letter' 93
'I'd like to spend long hours at home' 106
'I'd love to have you on a rainy day' 46
'If you have loved a brave story' 41
'If thou shouldst change, — become a god for me' 14
'I'm like all lovers, wanting love to be' 72
'I'm sorry I'm so young who love you, dear' 11
In the Public Library 4
'In this little school' 98
'Into old rhyme' 63
Inventory 100
'Last night, in a dream, I felt the peculiar anguish' 117
Lawstudent and Coach 49
Learning Geography 105
Lie-a-bed 22
Little Ships 1
Love Celestial 129
"Love is not love …" 121
Lovers Parted [I] 108
Lovers Parted [II] 110
'My darling boy' [I] 15
'My darling boy' [II] 15
'My lovely pixie, my good companion' 63
'My mission in the world' 23
'My window pane is broken' 91

'Most people have a way of making friends' 108
Machinist's Song 54
Machinists Talking 51
Martha 112
Miss Mary Fairfax 96
Mortal Poems 82
'Nay, dear, and must our friendship always be' 21
New Window, St John's Hawksburn 113
Noli Me Tangere 20
'Now all the lovely days are past' 100
'Now I've been three days' 65
'Now you are dead do you race the wind' 32
'O city songs' 38
'O Day and Night' 27
'O flame that bloweth with the wind' 41
'O little plum tree in the garden, you're' 58
'O little year, cram full of duty' 31
'O lovely day' 23
'O man, O woman, grievest so?' 69
'O sweet and fair! These words are mine to use' 92
'O you, dear trees, you have learned so much of beauty' 116
'Oh, but September is the month of flowers' 66
'Oh hall of music, promise fair' 6
'Oh I wish that my hair were as satiny shiny' 7
'Oh man is great. Be great. Seek loveliness' 33
'Oh night, find shelter for him in thy robe' 20
'Oh, oh Rosalie' 37
'Oh, you have given me store of happy days' 22
'Oh you, my own, who have gone before' 29
'Once I could say pretty things' 42
'Once in the early morning' 16
'Once I thought my love was worth the name' 85
'One day she put two arms around me' 96
One Man's Meat 101
'On the grass in the oaktree shadow I lie' 14
'Ours was a friendship in secret, my dear' 30

133

"Our Vegetable Love"   55
'Over your dear head'   69
'Pat wasn't Pat last night at all'   115
'People sometimes tease me, saying'   7
Periodicity [I]   49
Periodicity [II]   51
Periodicity [III]   56
'Pink eucalyptus flowers'   86
Polytheist   120
Pruning Flowering Gums   119
'Raging winter wind'   33
Raiment   125
"Rather like an Amazon schooled by Athena"   2
Rebels   87
Rossetti's Sea-Spell   37
Ruffs for Hilda Esson   40
'Sad trees, black and brown'   16
'She has all Ireland in her blood'   69
'She hates the North wind'   28
Shop Keeper and Customer   101
'Sitting here daylong'   47
Separation   17
Skirt Machinist   75
Slayers of Love   94
'Somebody brought in lilac'   31
'Some happy people can see and hear him daily'   11
'Sometimes I am too tired'   62
'Sometimes I think the happiest of love's moments'   91
'Sometimes I watch you, mark your brooding eyes'   30
'Sometimes I wish that I were Helen-fair'   62
Street Music   89
Summer Lightning   19
'Tall trees along the road'   12
The Changing Hills   116
The Contest   67
The Dead Youth   30
The Electric Tram to Kew   24
'The God who made this universe'   59
'The hot winds wake to life in the sweet daytime'   31
The Immigrant   43

The Invisible People   52
'The love I look for'   60
The Melbourne Cup   70
The Moonlit Room   122
The Nuns and the Lilies   71
'The people have drunk the wine of peace'   92
The Psychological Craze   109
'There is a child's name that I want to say'   70
'There is no need of hurrying'   126
The Silent Dead   35
The Sisters   124
The Troop-ships   16
The Two Swans   53
The Tyrant   11
The Wife   125
'They are so glad of a young companion'   58
'They say — priests say —'   21
'They sent me pictures of the saints'   114
Th' Inconstant Moon   67
'This evening I'm alone'   56
'This is a pretty road'   84
'This year I have seen autumn with new eyes'   3
'Those must be masts of ships the gazer sees'   64
'Though I had lost my love'   12
Three Teachers   99
To an Idealist   39
'Today, in class'   95
'Today I saw'   45
'Today is rebels' day. And yet we work'   88
'Today they made a bonfire'   26
'Today when you went up the hill'   45
To E.B.   105
To Leslie   35
'To look across at Moira gives me pleasure'   89
'Tonight when woes are manifold'   86
'To Plato's dictum'   40
'Under the pier'   80
'Up in my room on my unmade bed'   54
'Verse wov'n of thought'   28
'We climbed that hill'   76

Weekend at Mt. Dandenong 28
'What were the good of stars if none looked on them' 130
'When day is over' 2
'When I am articled' 126
'When I get up to light the fire' 95
'When I go up to work the young blue sea' 104
'When my lover put the sea between us' 127
'Whenever I think of you, you are alone' 97
White Sunshine 117
'Why does she put me to many indignities' 36

Wind at Night 107
Work-girl's Holiday 48
'You and I' 29
'You are a dream woman' 26
'You are more fair than shadows are' 42
'You may have other loves' 66
'You want a lily' 85
'You, whom the grave cannot bind' 19
'You work all day in the boiling sun' 10
'You'll never love me' 13

CPSIA information can be obtained
at www.ICGtesting.com
Printed in the USA
LVHW08s0345031018
592226LV00007B/150/P